Coaching For Female Entrepreneurs:

How Life Coaching Can Improve Your Bottom Line

12 Expert Life Coaches Reveal Their Proven Secrets

Co-authored by members of the International Association of Professional Life Coaches®

Compiled By Jeannette Koczela

Table of Contents

Forward

Female entrepreneurs have a different set of issues and challenges to deal with than male entrepreneurs. They may be homemakers who are inspired to open up shop; they may be mothers who have raised their children or are still raising them and want to work from home; or they may be retired and want to give back to the community. In any case, a woman entrepreneur still has to balance all of her life's activities with her work.

In the chapters of this book, you will read about our co-authors' experiences with coaching female entrepreneurs. They not only share their coaching methods but also the experiences of their clients and how they apply to female entrepreneurs.

Each chapter has gems of wisdom for female entrepreneurs, that will give insights, new techniques, and how life coaching can significantly improve your business and your bottom line.

Most entrepreneurs know that a business coach can help their business, however, they might not necessarily think to hire a life coach to help their business. But your business is part of your life, and your life absolutely affects your business.

As you read through these chapters, I hope this book gives you enough information and motivation to hire a coach for yourself.

You can find a listing of coaches, by category, to choose from in our Life Coach Directory at www.iaplifecoaches.org/life-coach-directory

I Believe Goethe Was Right ...
... So, No More Hesitation – Just Do It!
By Susie Briscoe

> *"Until one is committed, there is hesitancy, the chance to draw back ~ Concerning all acts of initiative (and creation), there is one elementary truth that ignorance of which kills countless ideas and splendid plans: that the moment one definitely commits oneself, then Providence moves too. All sorts of things occur to help one that would never otherwise have occurred. A whole stream of events issues from the decision, raising in one's favour all manner of unforeseen incidents and meetings and material assistance, which no man could have dreamed would have come his way. Whatever you can do, or dream you can do, begin it. Boldness has genius, power, and magic in it. Begin it now."*
> **- Johann Wolfgang von Goethe** 28 August 1749 – 22 March 1832)[1]

That is quite an opening for my chapter, yet when I stopped to consider what being a female entrepreneur is all about, Goethe's famous quote came to mind. Naturally, I believe that female entrepreneurs will require a coach and mentor as one of the givens in their life – well, given that I am an International Coach & Mentor I would do, wouldn't I? All successful people in the world have had a coach or mentor – and I'm not just talking here of the Olympic sports men and women ... I mean people like Presidents, Chairmen and CEO's of Blue Chip companies.

The coach/mentor is as necessary to your success as breathing in an out is to your life; it sits alongside your morning mug of tea or coffee and your power-bag containing all the necessities of today's busy business lives: smart phone; iPad; portable charger; neo smartpen; Tiffany rollerball; Smythson wee 'Ditzy' notebook and Fashion Diary, to name but a few.

Referring back to my chosen Goethe quote, we seldom see the entire quote; more often it is the last three sentences, with which we are more familiar.   But how often do we actually live by those words?

I decided to investigate this and see, when applying it to my clients lives as well as my own, how we came up short and then decided to create a formula that each of us can easily apply to make it happen … by Just Doing It!   Instead of thinking about it and procrastinating…   no more hesitation … and then I realize I'm quoting Nike's slogan! Suddenly, here we are with the 20th century sliding easily into the spirit still engendered today in the 21st century, alongside Goethe's 18th century noble words of wisdom. What is it that holds us back from claiming the success that is ours for the taking?

Here is some "housekeeping" to cover some of the basics:
1. Have you determined what you are good at?
2. Does this run alongside what you are passionate about?

It might be helpful for you to consider the pointers below to determine how close you are to your perfect ideal for working in complete synchronicity with your dreams…

I coach my clients to understand how essential it is to have the answer to these two questions in harmony, combined so that you are able to have your business run in a profitable as well as an enjoyable, fun, way. The important thing is that you are not feeling stressed about what you do… this will only attract negativity and most definitely will not bring the rewards of a healthy bottom line with which you will feel proud and comfortable to be associated.

There is absolutely no reason for you to go through life not living up to your full potential and thereby reaping the rewards that this will bring.   This is why it's essential to have a silent business partner looking over your shoulder, completely on your side, with no agenda of their own. Your Coach/Mentor in fact!   Who else is there to ask you difficult questions or guide you to look at and explore more options? Even to go and look for those out of the box ideas that can so easily come from brainstorming with someone who is absolutely there just for you? Team You! All the time.

So now I'm taking a leap of faith that you are actually working in your perfect circumstances in order to really take a deep look at how we, as females take stock of our bottom line financially speaking. If this isn't already your personal experience, then I have a solution for you, but more of that at the end of the chapter.

Do we think differently about our businesses to our male counterparts, or is this a fiction, which we still privately agree to allow, even contribute to, at a subconscious level? I believe that any difference is a perceived one only, as everyone in business will always want to keep a firm hand on the tiller when it comes to steering our professional efforts towards a healthy and reliable profit.

My first rule of engagement is that you identify your target market. We all speak easily about having a niche market. Again, it really is important to remember this: to build it a mile deep rather than a mile wide. There is so much space out there for all of us to have a lucrative business without feeling we are missing out on anything because we've gone deep rather than wide. The most experienced coaches and marketers all agree that this principle is what works for them and it will also work for you.

Having done this, the next rule is to always go for the lowest hanging fruit. I refer to what I call the 'money tree' as an example of how to approach the necessary 'bits' – this is obviously a very technical term! – that go to make up the various parts of your work, hence my reference to the lowest hanging fruit. I have my own 'rainbow' tree that I call on in my own business. What does this mean?

Let's pretend we are visiting an orchard in the autumn, just when the apples are ripening ready to be picked. There are apples all across the tree, on nearly every branch. Why would we not pick those apples that are the nearest and easiest to pick?   Why would we rather try to climb the tree or get a ladder – both a lot more effort – than be happy for those fruits, which are easily within grasp?   Is there some mythical legend that dictates only the ones out of reach will be the best, tastiest, and sweetest?   If that is the case I have to confess to not knowing that legend, but also confess to having been guilty of succumbing to this 'crime' in my business at some time or other!   The same applies to our businesses and by remembering to take the 'apples' that are within our grasp we will ensure a good harvest at the end of our financial year... this will also be a good rule of thumb with which to build your business.

What is it that you, as my client, are looking for when wanting to attract people to you in business?   What are you offering?   We have already worked out that you are precisely placed to work in your happiest context, so working with the people you most enjoy working with is an important next step in building your business. Now, confirm to yourself that you know your tribe and can identify where they hang out... what magazines they read, do they go to the spa or the gym – or both?   Are they on Facebook or LinkedIn... or both?   By identifying these habits alongside a host of other identifiable traits that these people will have, you are making it so much easier for yourself to get ahead.   Most often your client will be similar if not identical to you in your tastes and habits, so this gives you a head start as to know where to start looking for them.

Having found your tribe, you now need to communicate with them and provide them with things that they are falling over themselves to buy.   These days, so often we connect online via social media, email, that it makes it a whole lot easier and certainly a lot less expensive to send out mailings from your computer – so getting a potential client's email address is, of course, a vital part of the process.   Now that you have this, you are turning them from suspects into prospects with a better chance of them becoming loyal customers.

The word loyal is loaded: what is it that will make them become and then remain, loyal?   Superb customer service is one thing for sure, but before that the product or service itself has to be first class;

the *very* best you are able to provide on a continuing basis. The sad truth in today's market is that your reputation rests with client's mostly remembering their last transaction with you, so it is essential to make sure it is wonderful.

If things do go wrong, this is where you need to ensure that you react in the best way to maintain the relationship – remember how long and hard it was finding and then turning these people from suspects to prospects to clients or customers? The given strategy is that it takes a minimum of seven to twelve 'strokes' (think of stroking your pet) which, in this context, I mean to be communications from you of one kind or another, to even get your 'suspect' to recognize you are there – and that is a minimum number, remember – so having got their attention it is really well worthwhile to make sure that you go the extra mile here to ensure they remain happy. You will be well rewarded for your effort.

Having got your customers, and made sure that your business is growing, perhaps you are now ready to become brand conscious? A lot of mistakes occur when a business believes it has to have all the marketing and branding 'done' before they have sold anything. To me, it's more important to build the business and the brand will follow.

So now, maybe you want to consider getting the newsletter, that you send out regularly to your customers, reflects the same legend as your website – no matter what business you are in, as it is always good to keep yourself front of their mind in whatever way you can. Look at the colours you are using … are they the same or at least complimentary? The font you use in both – are they empathetic with each other? Small things matter and bring a cohesion to how people will subliminally remember you and it is this sort of detail which goes to making up your image; your brand.

Now that we are mentioning newsletters, it is the time to find the right autoresponder with which to work. There are so many to choose from, and I struggled with most of the ones I found. Personally, after some time deliberating, I decided that the one that had all the bells and whistles was the one for me at that stage of my business. It not only had the requisite autoresponder and kept all my email addresses (data) stored safely, but my final selection also included a shopping cart. In fact, this was what cinched the deal for me.

At first, I still thought I could do it on my own and for someone who is tech-savvy this would be the truth, but that isn't me. Although my chosen workhorse is easy to use, I still struggled more than I would have liked: I think it's a hereditary, histrionic autoimmune allergy to anything technical within myself! I simply don't like that aspect of my business. The simple solution was to get another pair of hands. I outsourced.

At what point do you think it might be wise to outsource? What do I mean by this. If you are a small business or even at the start-up stage we have been discussing, it would not necessarily make sense to employ someone full time. The business might not be able to stand this financial burden. However, if you are in the bricks and mortar world you might be able to get someone to work with you part time. The hours would be a given number and tasks would be firmly stated.

The same applies to online businesses. For example, I declare happily that I am averse to techie 'stuff" – another of those technical terms again – and when I realized just how long it took me to struggle to get a newsletter out (and I don't mean the writing of it – thankfully that comes with relative ease to me – but to get it into the auto-responder and actually programmed to mail) I recognized that there were more useful and financially rewarding tasks on which I could choose to spend my time. This is when I went Virtual Assistant (VA) shopping. I cannot tell you the relief when I found Anne, together with her own little army, who are now members of my team… part of my resources if you will. They take the strain; my 'stuff' looks better than presentable, definitely smart and professional because of their tender loving care and my clients just see the smoothly oiled machine which has become Acer Coaching Associates, aka me!

Your business is growing in a healthy and solid way, so now could be the time to start thinking outside of the box. What other ways are available to you to break new ground without rocking the boat? Who do you know who is offering a similar service to your own, that doesn't conflict with your own, but would enhance your offer? This is where you might want to joint venture to maximize your reach with services complementary to the ones you offer. For example, if you are a chiropractor or relaxation therapist, maybe think of getting together with another business that sells natural oils for massage, perfumed candles or bath bombs to help clients really relax and unwind.

In order to keep the growth going in your business, you will discover the need to employ other marketing tactics: blogging; writing articles for local and or national newspapers and magazines and e-zines; getting interviewed on radio stations; doing podcasts; writing e-books or a published book – the latter will certainly gain you credibility within your business world and makes a brilliant launch pad for your ongoing projects. Again, I would add that the benefit of having a coach working alongside you whilst you navigate your way through these opportunities for growth is exponential to the time it would take if you were to walk a solo pathway.

To get a stable income – one on which you can rely year on year with natural growth – you will need to devise ways to keep your audience interested. Have special launches, Facebook quizzes and advertising campaigns, fire sales, birthday and holiday deals; think creatively to see how you can divide the year up so that you have something happening each quarter, say, on which you can rely. When you take this approach, and have done this a few times you will be able to gauge how much money each one of these generated, and so if you are hitting a dry part of the year, then you will be able to refer to these strategies and use them accordingly to give your biz a boost.

The Universe likes to know how we are each doing. Remember to say thank you. Remember, also, to be clear about what you want to achieve next. No mixed messages. Just as our clients don't buy when they are in a muddle – a confused mind never buys – so it is with the Universe.   Decide what your next move is and be clear about how you envision this; how you think about it and how you verbalize your dreams and your wishes, is very important.

In all the excitement and flurry that goes with your own business it can be easy to get caught up in just what 'we' are doing.   I like to suggest to my clients that they always take time to celebrate how far they have come.   It is so important to always acknowledge your wins, no matter how small, and also remember to give back is just as vital.

I have been focused on charity work and contribution for most, if not all, of my adult life, so it has become a way of life.   When I'm working with clients I ask them to see how they could benefit someone or something other than themselves either within or outside their work life.   This leads to some amazing brainstorming and some interesting projects have emerged.   For example, one client is an image consultant and to start with was having difficulty in getting herself known.   We discussed several opportunities and she decided the one that would work best for her was selecting a charity with which she already had some affinity and offer to be the "cabaret" for a canapés and wine evening.   It soon grew like Topsy and before long we had involved 6 local fashion shops including a couple of male shops; then the local car sales-room heard about it and they wanted to celebrate the launch of a new car within their range.

When you are on the right path, everything seems to fall easily into alignment just like walking down a magic carpet, and once the car people were on board we then had not only the local newspapers and magazines, but also the national motoring press.   The venue changed several times from someone's drawing room, to the local village hall to the large car showroom with all the lighting and glitz you can imagine… very glamorous – I think you get the picture.   By thinking outside the box, we had managed to satisfy so many different angles for so many different people and at the same time raise a significant sum of money for her chosen charity as well as raising her own business profile.

Let us recap: my rules so far:

1. Decide what you are going to do and *Just Do It!*
2. Find a coach/mentor who is in alignment with your values and is not afraid to challenge you.
3. Confirm that you are working *in* and *to* your Passion, which will mean it never feels like work.
4. Identify your target market, then niche down within that market to make it your own whilst ensuring that there really is a need for what you're offering – that it's not just your fantasy that this will work!
5. Find your tribe and communicate with them regularly – not just selling but building rapport with them, sharing, appropriately, about you so that they will find a reason to want to continue the relationship.
6. Provide amazing service, products and customer care.
7. Look at your branding and marketing – are all your messages in alignment with your values, and is this flowing through from you to your website and into your newsletters?
8. Outsource: get an autoresponder service as well as extra pairs of hands when you need to lighten your load.
9. Market smart – think in terms of maximizing with minimal effort. Think out of the box: consider joint ventures to maximize your reach with services complementary to the ones you offer.
10. Remember to have gratitude and to give back. Develop a Legacy Mindset.

I was telling you earlier about my rainbow tree of gratitude. This is where I visit regularly inside myself. I check in to ensure that all that I am teaching my clients remains a Truth for me. I look at the list of things that I've shared above and check them off to maintain that I'm walking my own talk; that I'm being authentic in my teaching as well as my life.

I have a couple of options for you to get a flavour of what it would be like to have a coach in your life, and more truthfully not just any coach but me. Please see my biography and you will discover two gifts from me. The first one is the gift of downloading my self-study course, Be Bold!, and the other is a special offer to work with me privately on a one to one basis.

I very much look forward to learning more about you, and hope that you, too, will discover your own place to regularly have those vital private chats with yourself and check in to make sure you are walking your truth, in the same way that Goethe's words speak to me.

About the Author

Susie Briscoe – Founding Chair; Acer Coaching Associates International Business Lifestyle Coach & Mentor; Master Leadership with Legacy Mentor, Co-author of two #1 International Best Selling books: "Your Creative Thoughts" and "Ready, Aim, Thrive!"

An enthusiastic Corporate and Executive motivator, Susie is fervent about facilitating the developmental growth of clients and colleagues. Susie brings a wealth of life and business experience to her Client relationships: from her 40+ years in increasingly senior roles within the Corporate, Educational, Health and Charity environment, (as well as working at Senior Director levels across a business spectrum that covers industry, commerce, academia, professional bodies and government institutions both at National and International levels) she is well used to appraising, managing people and projects, coaching/mentoring/supervising to enhance performance, implementing new programs, and facilitating learning.

From Susie: I am so grateful to you for taking the time to choose this book for yourself or as a gift to someone you love – or both! – that I thought I would like to gift you something from my product list. I've chosen accordingly, to go with the sentiment of the book and my chapter it is entitled: **"Be Bold! Simple Steps To Building Your Confidence."**

When you lack confidence, you're putting yourself in jeopardy of losing the success you're capable of before you even begin to try.

This self-directed course guides you through the maze of building the confidence you need to get you through almost anything in life you're trying to accomplish. To download your gift, please go to: **www.tiny.cc/GiftFromSusie**.

I would also like to give you the opportunity of working with me at a special introduction rate only for readers of this book. I am offering a 30% reduction on my usual fee, so please go to **www.acercoachingassociates.com** to learn more about me and how we may work together, and **www.tiny.cc/schedulewithsusie** to select a time for a 30-minute non-obligation 'Get To Know You' session (writing IAPLC into the interview time slot selected), where we will explore how we might work together. I look forward to hearing from you.

Contact: briscoe1@freenetname.co.uk
www.acercoachingassociates.com
www.tiny.cc/schedulewithsusie
www.tiny.cc/GiftFromSusie

Relationships: An Important Factor To Your Business Success

By Lesli Doares

Companies are always looking for the latest advantage. Whether huge conglomerates or one-person start-ups, there seems to be a never-ending search for a competitive edge. The newest thing seems to be a focus on improving the emotional well-being of the workforce. In my view, this is both welcome and long overdue.

The long-known truth is that emotional health issues directly impact a company's business. They are the number one cause of lost productivity, increased absenteeism, and other indirect costs. Stress, depression, or anxiety often lead employees to take more sick days or simply muddle through the workday without performing at top capacity. And if you, as the CEO or sole employee, are the one experiencing these symptoms there is a real cost to the bottom line.

The Mental *HEALTH* Foundation defines EMOTIONAL HEALTH as "a positive state of wellbeing which enables an individual to be able to function in society and meet the demands of everyday life." It is the concept of paying attention to the state of mind and emotions and how that positively impacts one's overall ability to be productive and healthy.

This attention to emotional wellness as part of overall health has become so important that the federal government convened the National Committee on Workplace Emotional Wellness in 2010. They considered an emotionally healthy individual as someone who, in part:

- Feels that his/her basic needs are being met both at home and in the workplace.
- Is self-aware and accepts a wide range of feelings in self and others.

- Effectively arrives at personal decisions based upon the integration of feelings, cognition and behavior.
- Forms interdependent relationships based upon mutual commitment, trust and respect.

While all are important, the ability to form healthy, productive relationships is key. There is strong evidence that indicates that feeling close to, and being valued by, other people is a fundamental human need, and one that contributes to functioning well in the world, both professionally and personally.

This is because relationships are everywhere. They are the foundation of everything we do. Family, friends, clients, co-workers, colleagues — they're all a type of relationship. And the rules of relationships apply equally to them all.

We tend to think of relationships as being natural. After all, the very first relationship we're a part of happens without our having to do anything except exist. And kind of like breathing, which is also natural, relationships don't get much attention unless they become problematic.

But also like breathing, which happens unconsciously, we don't realize there are tools and skills that can make relationships easier and more satisfying.

I've learned this in a rather interesting way. For me, breathing in every day circumstances tends to go unnoticed. Put me in any kind of physical activity and I breathe backwards. In yoga, every time the instructor is breathing in, I'm breathing out. In ballet, I find myself holding my breath in the wrong places, which stops the natural flow of the movement. And when I lift weights in CrossFit, I also find myself breathing opposite to what is most effective. I believe this happens because my mind has to focus in too many places at the same time.

Being an entrepreneur is kind of like that. There is so much to pay attention to – the marketing, the cash flow, customer care and development, product creation, service delivery, and on and on and on. And, because you are a solopreneur or have a small team, most of this falls on your shoulders.

When you are focused on your business, I can almost guarantee that you aren't seeing your relationships as an important factor to your success. Yes, you might want more customers or clients. Yes, you might have a difficult employee situation that is taking your energy. But what is missing is the 30,000-foot view that your ultimate success is tied directly to your relationships. And not just the professional ones.

Think about it. The days that go really well are the ones in which all your interactions are positive and productive. The days that leave you exhausted and feeling uncertain are the ones where there was a difficult customer or a hard conversation with an employee or a family member. While you have the power to choose how you feel at any given moment, the type of contacts you have with others will influence your ability to do that.

Ultimately, this ability to determine your own emotional state and your corresponding actions is both powerful and liberating. Unfortunately, many of us, maybe even you, give this power over to others. We allow them to decide the course of the conversation or interaction and then are left feeling frustrated, resentful, and/or stressed. This is bad at the individual level but also for your business.

Claiming your power and owning your authenticity is all the rage now. What often isn't clear is how to do this. For women, this can be especially challenging. There are elements of relationships where women seem to have an edge. We have easy access to oxytocin, the bonding hormone. It is the basis for the "tend and befriend" response that allows for the formation of social groups. The presence of oxytocin results in a greater sense of calm in the face of stress--- a definite plus when trying to deal with deadlines and diverse groups of people.

In addition, women tend to be good listeners. We try to find connections between situations and people. This allows us to be empathic and enhance these connections.

As a result, we also tend to be more in touch with our emotions and intuition. While this can cause some problems when asked to provide logical reasoning, it creates a space for others to feel validated and supported. This ability to provide a collaborative environment is increasingly valued in all walks of life.

These skills are gaining greater acceptance as women gain ground in business. But this ability to tap into the emotional aspect of a situation has some challenges as well. Feelings are often viewed as subjective and not as reliable as logical reasoning. But feelings and intuition are nature's way of determining safety in a timely fashion when slower cognition can be detrimental. I've discovered that the times I ignored my feelings—my inner voice--are the times I have found myself in trouble.

Like most things in life, it isn't a question of either/or, logic or intuition. It's the necessity of both/and. The challenge is not putting all your eggs in either basket but knowing how to create balance between the two. It's in this delicate dance that a lot of the challenges reside.

Being able to relate to another person's struggles can lead to difficulties for you and your business. Identifying the value of your work and feeling comfortable with your price structure is one way this can show up. When a potential client "can't afford" the service or is late paying, there often is a pull to offer a discount or give an extension to ease their pain (and quite often, to be honest, yours).

Another way is in the handling of an unproductive employee, support service, or supplier. Receiving payment from you is something they count on and taking it away doesn't feel good. This is especially true if there hasn't been an egregious mistake made. So, instead of being upfront about the business needs or your reasonable expectations, you make do with a less- than ideal situation because loyalty and connection are important. Being seen as "nice" is often a nicely clothed anchor that women wear around their necks. This comes at a cost to efficiency, profit, and peace of mind.

These difficulties can also show up on the home front. Your partner may not be as supportive of your business as you would like. They don't fully understand the demands that come with being an entrepreneur. Or maybe you feel pulled by the never-ending tasks of running a house or being a parent. Because it's accepted that it's your job to make everyone else's life easier, you keep taking on more and more. You end up working two full-time jobs with neither one getting your best, and feeling resentful on top of it all.

The concept of "having it all" has been presented as the norm for women for so long that it's no longer questioned. But maybe it should be. So many contradictory messages about having both a successful career and family while neither disappointing others nor being selfish about going after your dreams are flying around that it's not surprising to get knocked off course by a few of them.

This is exactly what my client Rebecca was dealing with. A CPA with her own firm, Rebecca was struggling. Both she and her husband were entrepreneurs. He had a seasonal business, which made their income fluctuate wildly throughout the year. She felt a lot of pressure to bring in enough income to smooth out the valleys.

One way she sought to do this was to lower expenses. She let her mom use some space in the office for her own business and to let her help manage the office during the busy times. What Rebecca forgot to take into account was her mother's sometimes prickly personality and their own, often challenging, relationship. Her mother's physical health wasn't great, so there were lots of days missed and times when Rebecca needed to step in and get her mom to the doctor. In addition, her mother would countermand Rebecca's priorities to her staff. Not to mention, her mom would frequently trigger the office alarm and Rebecca was being charged fines for those false alarms.

All of this actually ended up costing Rebecca more in money, time, and stress. As we worked through it, Rebecca recognized her difficulty in establishing clear boundaries. While she did a fairly decent job with her staff, she soon realized this challenge also extended to dealing with her husband's ex and one of his children.

A deeper dive revealed that Rebecca was a "people pleaser". This was the identity she assumed as both the child of an alcoholic father and a distant mother. She was the glue that held her family together and, as long as she kept everyone else happy, life made sense. It was only after she started her own business that it became impossible to keep all the balls in the air.

Something had to give, and she realized it was her financial stability and emotional well-being. Faced with the choice between bankruptcy or establishing functional boundaries with her mother, she made the toughest choice possible for a "people pleaser" — she chose herself.

I'm sure you can hear the societal voices screaming, "But that's selfish". I know I can; and often do.

That's the flip side to the "people pleaser" coin. If you do anything that is even slightly self-focused, you are selfish. Anytime I hear this, I'm reminded of the part of the safety demonstration that flight attendants give about putting on your own oxygen mask first if you're traveling with someone who might need your help. It's not selfish to make sure you're okay so that you're available to assist others. Putting yourself, and your needs, goals, and desires, into the equation is not selfish. You're only selfish if you only consider yourself and not the impact on those around you.

But getting to this place is not easy, especially for women. Those twin manipulators, guilt and blame, are powerful foes. Subduing them is just another drain of energy and focus, especially if you feel you're fighting them all alone.

And, unfortunately, sometimes the sources of these antagonists are the very people you are counting on to have your back. Unless these relationships offer you real support, it's hard to have the capacity to keep moving forward.

The Necessary Solution

The simple answer to this, as my client Rebecca discovered, is to value yourself. Not more than you value others, but not less either. The truth is that no one can make you feel guilt or blame without your cooperation. So, if you feel either, the source is inside. Gain control of this and success will be able to follow. As Eleanor Roosevelt stated, "In the long run, we shape our lives, and we shape ourselves. The process never ends until we die. And the choices we make are ultimately our own responsibility."

One choice that is absolutely essential to this process is the creation and enforcement of boundaries. Being clear and consistent about what is acceptable, and what is not, lets everyone know where he or she stands. The level of ease and comfort you feel with this process will determine your success and satisfaction in life.

Establishing clear and reasonable boundaries isn't something you do to other people. It's something you do for yourself. Locking your car or your house is a form of protection. Creating personal and professional boundaries is no different. They just take more thought and intention to implement effectively. This is because everyone understands and, to a degree, accepts locks. Many, however, will push back against your boundaries, no matter how rational and evenhanded. Being prepared for this certain reaction is the way to counteract it.

The clearer the roles of each person, the more likely boundaries will be honored. If you're the boss, you get to make the rules. Your employees might not like them but will either accept them or leave. The same is true of your clients or customers. But only if you're clear. The blurrier the roles, the blurrier the rules.

Boundaries are just as necessary in your personal life. Establishing them may just be more difficult because the roles aren't as well defined, and the perceived stakes are higher. The fear of losing a customer, while real, is manageable. The fear of losing a partner or alienating a family member can be devastating. So, you hedge. You ask for their permission to set a boundary or you back down when they push against it. Then feel frustrated and taken advantage of afterward.

Setting boundaries is uncomfortable because of the natural pushback that is interpreted as conflict—something most of us would rather not deal with. But the result of a lack of boundaries is an increase in conflict, not less. The truth is that perceived conflict can't really be avoided, only postponed. The longer it is unaddressed, the harder it is to resolve.

There are two important ways to address this. First, change the definition of conflict.

Any two people are going to disagree about something at some point. This is a simply a function of their different life experiences. Just because it is difficult doesn't mean it's bad. It will only turn into conflict if that's how it's defined.

The second way to address it is to become a master of communication. Without effective communication, setting boundaries is impossible which makes good relationships unattainable. Just as relationships provide the underpinnings of emotional health, good communication is their necessary foundation.

In the same way that relationships are considered natural in that they have always been there, communication is seen through the same lens. And it suffers from the same distortions. We start talking as babies and those around us work hard to figure out what we want. When they fail, frustration and distress are the result. This pattern continues through childhood until the expectation gets deeply engrained that it's up to others to understand what we're trying to say. When they don't, often the response is to blame, get angry, become defensive, and/or withdraw. The greater the expectation for the other person to "just know" what you mean, the more intense your negative response will be when they don't.

The biggest problem is that instead of being taught the techniques and given the tools to communicate effectively, you learn by trial and error. Because you haven't been given the skills or a method to implement them, you get stuck doing the same things repetitively yet hoping for a different result. With each unsuccessful interaction, the level of frustration and futility increases, and so does the perception of conflict. As a result, your relationship with that person suffers.

Here's the good news. While disagreements will happen, arguments and conflict are choices. And, because they are choices, you are in control of whether or not they occur. This is where your power lives. Understanding your part in the pattern, and learning to behave in a different way, is the path to a different, more pleasant outcome. And the best part is that you don't need the other party's consent or even their awareness to pull it off.

Now I didn't always know this. Growing up, I fought with one of my sisters practically every day. She would purposely provoke me, and I would take the bait every time. I got really good at fighting because I thought I had to, not just to be heard, but to survive.

Unfortunately, I took that mindset into many of my relationships with not-good results. The more things were going wrong, the more I gave my power away, the less secure I felt, the more I fought. What I didn't understand is that the more I fought, the more I was inviting the end of the relationship. Luckily, something happened that changed this for me.

One day, my very easy-going husband asked me a life-changing question. He said, "When you get upset, would you mind not taking a flamethrower to everything in your path?" Meaning him. Now, I had been a marriage therapist for over five years when he asked this, and I thought I had this relationship communication thing down. But, in that moment, I recognized that if I didn't start doing things differently, I would bring about the end of my marriage. For a child of divorce, and the mother of two children, this was completely unacceptable. It also meant I wasn't going to be effective in my business.

As a result of this "aha" moment, and a lot of work with my clients, I have developed a strategy to help people take control of their conversations.

In my 5 Steps to Conflict-Free Communication, I present the communication skills that are essential for having healthy, productive relationships in all aspects of your life. The steps are:

1. **Composure** – Being in control of your emotions and reactions is the critical first step to effective communication. Learning to identify your triggers and manage your reactivity are necessary skills to keeping a conversation from turning into an argument. It is impossible to listen or think clearly when the body is flooded with emotion. Unfortunately, this is the time when many challenging conversations are initiated.

2. **Clarity** – Being clear about both the purpose of the conversation and the real topic is fundamental to its success. Many misunderstandings occur because the two of you aren't actually talking about the same thing. In addition, knowing what you want to accomplish will serve as a guide to what you say and how you say it.

3. **Comprehension** — Removing ambiguity about both what is being said and heard is crucial to reaching resolution. This not the same as needing to understand or agree with it. There are several tools that can help illuminate each of your positions while minimizing antagonism and defensiveness.

4. **Compassion** –Being able to accept that you each have different perceptions and life experiences is pivotal to a successful outcome. Feeling heard and being validated are necessary components of respect. Having to justify or defend yourself are not. The ability to be empathic is the essential skill at play here.

5. **Connection** – This final step is tied directly to Compassion. It involves the openness of your approach. Being able to invite the other person into the conversation requires establishing a safe space for an honest, yet gentle, sharing. Being willing and able to hear their "truth" is vital to the success of both the conversation and the relationship.

Mastering this step circles you back to the first one, Composure.

As you can see, effective communication is an on-going and interconnected process. Like an onion, it has multiple layers, so it is no wonder that many of us struggle with this "natural" process. It's also why having knowledge alone isn't enough to be truly proficient at it. I know it wasn't for me.

So, I ask you to take a moment and imagine how your life- both personal and professional- would be different if you were able to minimize the conflict in it. What could you accomplish if you had the tools and techniques to approach any conversation, no matter how challenging, with confidence and composure? How would your emotional health and well-being be impacted? And that of the people around you?

I can tell you, both from personal experience and years of working with my clients, that it can happen. It is possible to speak from your own power and authenticity, without raising your voice or asking permission. It is feasible to set clear boundaries, have them respected, and not be consumed with guilt when others want you to do something else. And, you don't have to do it alone.

So, are you ready to take charge of your conversations? Do you desire to have conflict be a thing of the past? Are you yearning to have healthy, successful relationships? If you are, all you have to do is let me know.

About the Author

Lesli Doares has had a life-long curiosity about what makes relationships work. Throughout her seemingly random career choices — brokerage firm, retail, corporate HR — this interest has been the constant. After professional study to become a Licensed Marriage and Family Therapist, having a private practice, and her personal experience as a wife and mother, Lesli has found some answers.

She presents her conclusions in her book "Blueprint for a Lasting Marriage: How to Create Your Happily Ever After with More Intention, Less Work". This simple five-step approach is a practical guide to designing a healthy, successful relationship.

Lesli's passion is for creating happy, successful relationships and reducing the chance of heartache. She is gifted at understanding and explaining the dynamics of relationships in a way that enables her clients to see the possibilities for theirs, no matter how discouraged they are at first. Her clients say she is an angel in disguise.

Lesli is approachable and open. Her clients feel listened to and understood, as she honestly and gently challenges them to think about their relationship in a new and different way. One former client says that when she and her husband reach an impasse, she still asks herself, "What would Lesli say?"

To get a copy of her free report, *"The Truth: Why You're Fighting and What to Do About It"* go to www.foundationscoachingnc.com

Website: www.foundationscoaching.com
Email: lesli@foundationscoaching.com

It's Never Too Late to Pursue Your Dreams

By Bob Fraser

Eighty percent of American workers are looking for another job. Many of them are happy with their income and health benefits but are unhappy because their work isn't meaningful and fulfilling.

Are you one of them?

Do you remember when you were younger, maybe as a teenager or young adult, dreaming of a career that would fuel your passion? For me, it was teaching.

I grew up in a neighborhood where most of the kids were 3-4 years younger than me, and I enjoyed teaching these younger kids how to play sports. Being a teacher felt natural to me, and I thought it was what I was supposed to do: it was my life's purpose.

Despite a reading disability and a fear of public speaking, I still wanted to be a teacher. I felt like teaching was God's calling for my life and at 15 years old, teaching was my dream.

During my senior year in high school, my only plans were to graduate from school and get a job -- any job -- just to make a living. I talked to the school guidance counselor to get some ideas for my future, and he suggested I pursue a trade instead of college because of my low grades. At this point in my life, I agreed because I had no interest in going to college.

From the time I was 16 to the time I was 38, I had over 20 different part-time and full-time jobs. I simply changed jobs for better hours and better pay. I also owned several small businesses, but none of these jobs or businesses had anything to do with my dreams or passion. They were simply a means to pay my bills.

When I was growing up in the late 1960's, getting a job was all about making good money and having good benefits. Finding work you loved was not part of the equation.

Many people have told me that their dreams were squashed by their parents or friends. Some of them wanted a career in music or art, but people told them it wasn't realistic. Activities like music or art make a good hobby, but not a good career choice, they said. Get a "real" job, they said.

Can you remember being told things like this? Maybe you shared your dream with friends and family members when you were younger, and they discouraged you from pursuing your dream job. They didn't think your dream career was practical. Maybe you heard them say, "That sounds nice, but you can't make a living doing that."

Sometimes our dreams are squashed by others' opinions or by our own feelings of inadequacy. If you are in your 30's or 40's and you've never pursued your dream, I want to assure you that it's not too late to live your dream.

In the last 10 to 15 years, attitudes among workers have changed, especially due to the advancement of the Internet. Every day, new online business opportunities and work-from-home job opportunities emerge. There is a mindset now that you *can* find or create work you love, and that you *should* pursue your dream job. It is possible to find work that is meaningful, fulfilling, and profitable that aligns with your desires and passions.

If you can't find your dream job, then create it! Some people have established online businesses by creating dog training videos, teaching guitar lessons online and developing many other businesses that fulfill their passions. This simply wasn't possible 10 to 15 years ago.

I didn't pursue my dream of being a teacher until I was 38 years old.

In February of 1989, I had an amazing encounter with God. I was living life like the prodigal son in the Bible, but that day, I could sense God's presence. He wanted me to change the way I was living and follow Him again. In an instant, my life transformed into one of peace and purpose.

The next day I told my brother what happened, and he said God was giving me a second chance in life.

"Every day is the first day of the rest of your life," my brother said. "What are you going to do about it?"

I didn't have to think about it very long; I wanted to follow my passion and calling and be a teacher. The next week I enrolled in school to pursue a teaching career.

After four and a half years, I started my teaching career at the age of 43. It was something I had to do, and I had never felt that way about anything else in my life.

I taught school for 14 years and loved living out my passion. I continue to live out my passion today as a life coach helping other people pursue their dreams, passion, and purpose for life.

At the end of our lives, our biggest regrets won't be the things we did wrong, but the things we didn't do. Stop living in the past and thinking it's too late to pursue your dreams because it's never too late. It's your turn to pursue your passion.

What is God calling you to do?

What does it take to be a successful entrepreneur?

You must have a passion for what you want to do.
Don't start a business just to make money. Most successful business owners are passionate about what they do. Passion will keep you from giving up when things get hard. It takes time to build a business, and if you have passion, you will keep going.

You must be passionate about serving others. In any business you operate, you will be serving others, whether it's a service business, a restaurant, or a retail store. If you don't like what you are doing, you will not be successful.

You must have a vision.
You must have a vision for your business. What will your business and life look like when you achieve your vision? Create a vision and mission statement for your business and work at fulfilling your vision. If you have employees, hire people that share your vision.

Identify your unique skills and abilities.
What are you good at and how can you use your skills and talents to help or serve others? You have skills that are transferable to other types of careers; skills that you can use to start your own business. What skills and desires can you combine with your passion?

Set goals in order to be successful.
You must have formalized goals. Otherwise, you don't have any idea where you are heading and you won't realize it when you get there. Start out with a 5-year plan then make short-term goals to reach your 5-year goal.

Goal setting helps you in several ways. First, according to a study done at Yale University, it helps you succeed dramatically. Secondly, goals govern your whole approach to achievement. A clear vision and goal structure cut through indecision. Third, goal setting contributes to a healthier lifestyle. Most stress comes from confusion and fear. Goals also help to provide a sense of accomplishment.

Make S.M.A.R.T. goals; goals that are specific, measurable, attainable, relevant and time-based.

Know your audience.
Is there a market for your products or services? If so, you must identify them and find the best way to market to them. Are they on Facebook, Linkedin, or some other social media? If they spend most

of their time on Facebook but you market on Twitter, you will waste your time and money.

You must know who your potential customers are and where to find them. What age group are you targeting? Are they single or married? Do they have children? The more specific you can be about your ideal customer, the more successful you will be.

Be willing to learn from your mistakes
There are risks in starting your own business. Some things you try will work, and some things will fail. Learn from the things that fail so you don't repeat the same mistakes.

Establish systems before hiring employees.
When your business starts to grow, and you need people to help you, put systems in place. Systems will allow your business to function without you. Your goal should be to work *on* your business and not *in* your business. Establishing systems for your business will allow you freedom. Once you train people to follow your systems, the business will operate without you being present.

Find a mentor or coach.
A life coach can help you transition from an unfulfilling job to your dream job. A life coach will help you clarify your desires. A coach will help you focus on reaching your goals and will keep you accountable to your goals.

Many life coaches transitioned to coaching because of their passion for helping others find their dream job. Many spent time in careers they weren't happy in, so they understand your predicament. Many life coaches hire their own life coaches to help them stay focused and accountable. Many coaches also belong to support groups, like Mastermind Groups, which offer encouragement and help them overcome obstacles.

I have a personal coach, and I belong to a Mastermind group. Whenever I get discouraged the people in my Mastermind Group help me get clarity and encourages me. I always feel uplifted after meeting with them. My coach gives me advice and helps when I create emails and promotions by critiquing my work before I publish it.

Working with a coach can be beneficial because coaches understand your desire to pursue your passion and live the life of your dreams. Friends and family may not understand why you want to make a change, especially if you have a secure job with a good salary and benefits.

The job of a life coach is to listen, ask questions, identify goals, offer an outside viewpoint, hold you accountable, and work with you to develop strategies for overcoming your roadblocks and struggles.

Having an accountability partner like a coach is a good investment of your time and finances. Hiring a life coach is not simply an expense; it is an investment in your future.

Coaching addresses your entire life and helps you find balance and live according to your beliefs, ethics, morals, hopes, and dreams. Your goal should be to plan your work and business around your life, rather than planning your life around your work.

A good coach will listen to what the client wants to achieve. A coach will listen for self-doubt, uncertainty and limiting beliefs that the client expresses. A coach will ask questions to clarify what might be holding you back from achieving your dream. Coaches listen beyond the content for language patterns that undermine your self-confidence.

If you want to be successful, don't do it alone. Get help from someone who understands, who will listen, who will encourage you when you feel like giving up, and who will help you overcome the tough times.

About the Author

I'm a Career and Business Coach. I pursued my dream, and I would like to help you pursue your dream. I have also owned five small businesses in the past 30 years. I can share marketing strategies that worked for me, some of which cost very little or nothing to implement.

I can help you achieve your goals.

I offer personal, one-on-one coaching, group coaching, and a Mastermind Group where you'll find support from other people that are on a similar journey of pursuing their dream. You can also join my private Facebook Group for support.

I also offer a free 30-minute Discovery Session. During this time, I will find out what your goals are and I'll share more about myself so we can determine if we are a good fit to work together.

Additionally, I wrote a book about my life story called *God Met Me at The Mailbox*, available on Amazon.

Visit my website for a free report, "5 Strategies for Finding Your Dream Job", this report will also help you to decide on what kind of business you should start.

Bob Fraser
Career & Business Coach
bob@bobmfraser.com
 www.bobmfraser.com
For a FREE 30-minute, Discovery Session click here
https://my.timetrade.com/book/YTJPC

Lifelong Learning, Leading and Meaning for Female Coaches and Women Entrepreneurs
By Rudy Garrity

Insights on Women Entrepreneurs and Female Coaches

Over the last 15 years there has been a steady increase in women deciding to strike out on their own not only in coaching but also in numerous fields open to entrepreneurial skills. Some of this has certainly been due to the ups and downs in the economy, but much has changed in the American culture as the female gender, in large measure, has become more educated and proactive in deciding to participate more directly in the business marketplace. What everyone appears to be acknowledging through this experience is that innovation and change does require an openness to new ways of thinking, learning, relating and providing service.in a "time is of the essence world" -- especially when impatience and stress have become prevalent in our culture. My theme of society progress through lifelong learning (my American Learnership trademark) has been extended to include learning one's own (and client's) purpose and meaning early in their personal and career relationships.

A professionally certified coach, whether man or woman, has chosen to be of personal service to other members of their community. The knowledge, skills and abilities used when performing coaching services are usually a blend of cognitive and emotional talent in which the client's situation and needs are discerned before alternatives are developed and action is planned and initiated. Quite often, a significant percentage of women choose to pursue personal, family, social and life coaching as a career (perhaps as much as 75 percent), than do men who probably represent a higher percentage in coaching sports activities.

Regardless of gender, coaches are expected to be willing and proactive learners, who assess situations, develop knowledge, lead client learning and motivation towards positive outcomes. Additionally, this work finds itself valued to the degree that clients report themselves as becoming more grounded, knowledgeable and able to manage their issues and illnesses. It has been said that the one-on-one coaching done by women is enhanced by the likelihood of the greater patience and understanding they reveal as well as their emphasis on relationship building and demonstrated empathy.

Learning and Learnership™

Learning is a process that is the cornerstone of all human activity. Without learning, there is no human growth and development – personhood is not possible. And, at the microscopic level, the genes of the human genome – the foundational recipes for both our anatomy and behavior – cannot develop without exposure to and influence from their human (host) environment (Genome, 1999, by Ridley). It is a fact that life itself depends upon the ability of the human organism to learn from the interaction of its ingrained predispositions (nature) and its experience with its surroundings (nurture). The ability for our genes to evolve is based on their capacity for microscopic change and mutation. For complex human beings, our ability to learn and develop is tightly linked to our capacity and willingness to engage, understand, and accommodate our environment. Norman Vincent Peale said: *"The successful person is always a learner'*.

Learners are people with an ability to learn, which makes everyone to some degree a learner. Most of us fail to learn to excel at the pace, depth, breadth and length of time required to be categorized as first rate learners. To continually discover new, worthwhile and satisfaction-giving topics requires learners committed to open, inquisitive, proactive and action-oriented ways of learning. Their cognitive and emotionally based modes of sensing/thinking, interpreting/deciding, and realizing/acting need coherent interplay with their personal attributes. Good learners are able to learn effectively within the context of increasing time constraints, constant change, and the increasing complexity of modern life. Learning is essential for knowing.

Knowing is a capability that results from learning. Efficient and effective learners know more useful information about the people, things, and situations in life that matter. Learners and learning are focused on knowledge and knowing. In particular, having in our brains (or at our disposal) the information and knowledge required to understand, plan, execute, and reflect on our life activities incrementally advances growth and development. Knowing is essential for achieving. Gail Sheehy said: *"The secret of a leader lies in the tests he has faced over the whole of his life and the habit of action he develops in meeting those tests"*.

Leading is a process that has to do with our ability to use our knowledge to influence others' thinking and behavior. Because learning creates change, leading is also essential if the new state of knowledge is to be shared and actualized. The process of leading change includes creating a future vision, building a case for change, involving important stakeholders, and implementing compelling improvements – all of which should demonstrate the viability of the new knowledge and encourage early adaptation by those affected. Without effective leading little is accomplished – much like racing the engine on a high performance car but never putting the vehicle in gear. Leading is essential for putting knowledge into action. John Quincy Adams, 6th President of the United States, once said: *"If your actions inspire others to dream more, learn more, do more, and become more, you are a leader"*.

Leadership, the distinguishing characteristic of leaders is that they are able to get others to travel to an unfamiliar location, accomplish a desired objective, or change a personal perspective without fully knowing all the information that might be relevant.

Leaders create a sense of direction, motivation and trust in others so that their personal thoughts, needs or plans are considered and action is taken. Some of the traits positively correlated with effective leadership include being competent, focused, fair, objective and friendly; having a positive attitude, and showing good initiative.

Building and Using a Lifelong Learning and Leadership (Learnership) Architecture

Ralph Waldo Emerson once said, "Life is a succession of lessons which must be lived to be understood." Of course, the problem here is that by the time we live long enough to understand what is worth knowing, it is often too late to chart an informed course of action meaningful for the life we are now living.

How then is it possible to capture the wisdom of exemplars – borne of time, experience and reflection – and make knowledge both discoverable and usable in our expanding, fast-paced world? Is there an agile but systematic process for thinking, learning and knowing that can empower more of us to discover our unique purpose and to accomplish our respective goals, needs and contributions?

The premise of this chapter is that we can learn to manage ourselves – and to even lead others in their own development – towards the intellectual and emotional maturity that makes significant personal accomplishment probable. And, this may be done regardless of our personal histories or social status. The theoretical construct through which this occurs has three major propositions:

1. That systems thinking, pattern recognition, situational learning, knowledge management, and adaptive leadership are foundational mental activities that serve as building blocks for managing what is worth thinking, learning, knowing, leading, and pursuing to select and achieve a holistic set of life goals.

2. That to understand and accomplish these life goals, an architecture

consisting of the five competencies and four interdependent social systems requires our thoughtful reflection. These social systems consist of our personal social system, our organizational social system, our community social system, and our perspective on societal social systems among nations and geopolitical networks.

3. That the concurrent use and integration of the five reasoning competencies and four social systems allows those so inclined to achieve a mindful way-of-being. That is, they become skilled in their ability to dynamically process information and confident that knowledge acquired is relevant to their needs.

Figure 1 illustrates the relationship among these major reasoning competencies, system-of-systems, and human aspiration to "get our minds around matters essential in our lives. Ideally, these interdependent systems are developed and applied in a balanced manner with due consideration for personal, organizational, and community needs and responsibilities.

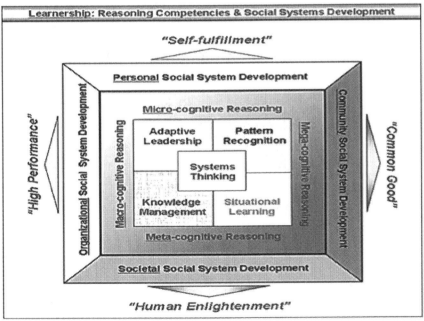

Figure 1

Building Reasoning Competencies

The practice of learnership emphasizes five critical competencies that enable us to reason more efficiently and effectively, and to become more emotionally and psychologically balanced. Specifically, they enable us to better manage our thinking, learning, knowing, leading and goal-seeking activities. These competencies serve as catalysts in our efforts to manage and improve our performance in the four major social systems we inhabit – the personal, organization, community and societal social systems of life. The competencies are defined below, and are then succeeded by descriptions of the four interdependent social systems they enable.

1. System Thinking (ST). A system perspective on social matters that illustrates the interdependency and mutual support among the personal, organizational, and community subsystems within which we learn, develop, and strive for success. The system thinking competency helps us develop a broader, more integrated outlook, and to expand the contextual environment of our thoughts and decisions.

2. Pattern Recognition (PR). By definition, a pattern can be an archetype, a model, an ideal worthy of imitation, a representative sample of something, or a composite of traits or features charac-teristic of individuals. All biological life forms maintain and exhibit patterns of activity; and, the social development of humankind is inextricably anchored to our thought processes as revealed in our behavior.

3. Situational Learning (SL). A major life activity is dealing with the wide variety of situations we encounter on a daily basis. Some situations are routine and need little attention while at the other end of the continuum they may be significantly life and/or career threatening. What is important to understand is that every situation we encounter requires some amount of information gathering and analysis followed by decision-making and action.

4. Knowledge Management (KM). Human development can only

proceed as far as our combined knowledge will allow. Whether we view ourselves as individuals, organizations or communities, we are both empowered and constrained by our current knowledge, and our willingness and ability to acquire additional knowledge. Contemporary studies and writings indicate that knowledge may be systematically created, managed and used to enhance human development and to produce the products and services we need and desire.

5. Adaptive Leadership (AL). No amount of knowledge has practical value until it is applied to human needs or concerns. Someone needs to articulate what is known, show relevancy to the situation or challenge at hand, and propose a course of action that can create a meaningful result. It is the work of leaders to craft visions and futures that inspire others to accept change and become participants in the journey forward.

Using Reasoning Competencies for Social Systems Development

1. Personal Systems Development (PSD). PSD is social synthesis at the micro-cognitive level, and is the starting point for managing the quality of our individual lives. Priority at this level is focused on continuous improvement of our health, character and ability. The universal goal selected for individuals is *self-fulfillment*, and the key role to be played is that of *fellowship*. Learning, knowing, and leading inform and activate PSD.

2. Organizational Systems Development (OSD). OSD is social synthesis at the macro-cognitive level, and uses recognized benchmarks for achieving highly efficient and effective organizational performance. The organizational elements selected for intense management focus are the organization's direction, operations and performance. The universal goal selected for organizations is *high performance*, and the key role to be played is *leadership*. Learning, knowing, and leading inform and activate OSD.

3. Community Systems Development (CSD). CSD, is social

synthesis at the mega-cognitive level, and is conceived as the pathway for experiencing a rewarding community life. The community elements under development at this level are the institutions of government, education and business. The universal goal selected for communities is the *common good*, and the key role to be played is *citizenship*. Learning, knowing, and leading inform and activate CSD.

4. <u>Societal Systems Development (SSD)</u>. SSD is social synthesis at the meta-cognitive level, and consists of fully integrated reasoning and development across all four levels of social synthesis. SSD strives to capture the spirit of John Sullivan's *To Come to Life More Fully* (1990), and suggests milestones for our timeless journey towards holistic personhood. The universal goal selected for the societal level is *human enlightenment*, and the key role to be played is *statesmanship*. Learning, knowing, and leading inform and activate SSD. (Reference Figure 1)

Achieving Mindful Coaching and Leadership Skills
Learnership practitioners are people who systematically increase their understanding of life's opportunities and challenges; develop their skills through questioning and learning; and produce products and services of value to themselves and others. They are knowledge managers in that they continually identify, acquire, organize, use and share new found knowledge within their respective social systems. They learn and lead within their personal domains, they develop and apply knowledge practices and tools in their organizational roles, and they contribute as informed problem-solvers within their local communities.

Using lifelong learning, they seek to optimize the integration of their personal self-fulfillment, organizational high performance, the community common good and societal human enlightenment. They may even experience what Csikszentmihalyi (*Flow*, 1990), Senge et al (*Presence*, 2007), and Langer (*Mindfulness*, (1989) have eloquently described in their well-regarded writings. Learnership practitioners who are also coaches and entrepreneurs should expect to experience vibrant and rewarding coach-client and leader-customer-outcomes.

Discovering the Meaning of Your Life
In the pursuit of learning and knowing what we term our *"meaning"* it is essential that we understand that while "meaning" is often thought to be something dynamic we objectively demonstrate outside ourselves, in fact, "meaning" always begins inside ourselves as our worldview of appropriate beliefs, values, motives and preferred actions before we reveal them to others.

Female coaches need to be astute in understanding their own purpose and meaning in life, and then be able to determine whether their clients need assistance in building a foundation of support in this important human function. Similarly, women entrepreneurs need to be astute observers of their business climate and the accepted purposes and practices in their respective fields.

Our own pre-programmed and ingrained belief system established in our brain tells us what and who we are – and whether the time has come to share and declare ourselves to others. And, because we all have different brain stores of data, images, beliefs and values it is certain that variations of "meaning" exist even among those who say they are committed to the same "meaning." Knowing this enables coaches to maintain a balance between their own and their clients' expectations of near and longer term objectives and outcomes.

Figure 2

In his book *Re-Create Your Life* (1997), author Morty Lefkoe says that our consciousness creates our own realities, and he encourages us to occasionally set aside our beliefs long enough to consider a different way for viewing our lives. In doing so we should apply five well accepted principles:

1. Existence is a function of consciousness.

2. Language is the primary tool we use to make distinctions.

3. There is no inherent meaning (or "the truth") in the world.

4. When you create a belief, you create your reality.

5. When you eliminate a belief, you change your reality and create new possibilities.

The importance of this cognitive activity is that when we search for, and think about, meanings that are central to our existence; and prioritize them for use of our intellect and resources we should do so in an informed manner. Accuracy, efficiency and effectiveness all matter in accomplishing this fundamentally personal responsibility.

There is a learning process and decision-making activity required for each of us to say with conviction that "this is what I believe; this is my meaning in life; this is how I make my decisions; this is what motivates me; and this is how I manage myself, contribute to others and impact the world." Engaging this topic from a variety of viewing points allows us to clarify our personal meanings and make better choices that influence our unique sense of self, vision, mission and personhood.

Maslow's Hierarchy of Needs and Motivation

Abraham Maslow presented his hierarchy of human needs ranging from *Physiological Needs* at the bottom to *Self-Actualization* needs at the top – with the other three needs *Safety, Love and Belonging,* and *Esteem.* It is not known whether he ever actually presented that information in a pyramid as illustrated in Figure 3. What is notable is that he referred to the lowest needs as *deficiency needs* with the belief that a lack of physical capabilities and sufficient safety, love and belonging, and esteem – if not corrected over time – would limit one's ability to achieve self-actualization. A short definition of each need follows: (Figure 3)

1. Physiological Needs – These are the physical requirements for human survival. This has to be minimally satisfied for any progress to a higher level.

2. Safety Needs – These needs are also very basic and include personal security, financial security and health and well-being.

3. Love and Belonging – These needs are interpersonal and involves feelings of belongingness. They become more important as the lower two needs are adequately met.

4. Esteem – This need emerges as the three lower needs are met and a person becomes more independent due their lower three needs being met to a reasonable degree.

5. Self-Actualization – This need or desire becomes a greater force

as a person overcomes major deficiencies the four lower levels of the hierarchy, and even masters them so at level 5 one can focus on becoming "all that he or she desires to become."

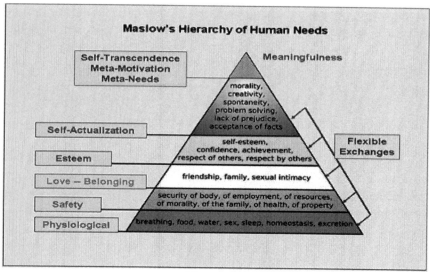

Figure 3

Due to his seminal work, Maslow is still highly regarded even though many respected researchers and psychologists have updated or modified his work as they expanded the range of psychology and sociology knowledge using more modern methods and tools. One area of interest concerns obvious differences between people raised in individualistic (self) cultures and those raised in collectivist (others) cultures.

To appreciate Maslow's theory completely, Figure 3 in this text places emphasis on two additional aspects of his theory. The first is the addition to the model of "flexible exchanges" which is meant to emphasize individuals may be significantly different as to their psychological preferences, cultural upbringing or stage of development in which they currently reside. It may be that we can temporarily subsume certain lower level need in order to emphasize a higher level need. We can make changes as the circumstances we are in take a dramatic turn. The model depicts a theory for most normal situations, but is not predictive for everyone.

A second added feature of the model is particularly important for use in this chapter. This is shown as a capstone added here on top of Maslow's hierarchy. As Maslow's work matured he recognized that only a minority of exceptional people in any society or nation could achieve a high degree of self-actualization. So what, then, could they expect and experience going forward?

His view was that *meta-needs* would develop, leading to *meta-motivation*, and culminating in *self-transcendence*. He said that once a person had navigated his hierarchy of needs, and substantively accommodated them, they were now willing to travel a new path of their own making to achieve self-directed growth. For purposes of this chapter, a high level summary of what might be termed "Universal Ideals" has been compiled from multiple philosophical sources and is presented as a reference for depicting the breadth of Maslow's Meta-needs.

Universal Ideals	Maslow's Meta-needs
Truth – Honesty	Truth (reality)
	Simplicity (essence)
Beauty – Goodness	Beauty (rightness of form)
	Goodness (benevolence)
	Perfection (harmony)
	Wholeness (unity)
	Richness (complexity)
Freedom – Democracy	Autonomy (self-sufficiency)
	Liveliness (spontaneity)

Justice – Equality	Justice (fairness)
	Uniqueness (individuality)
Love – Happiness	Playfulness (ease)
Responsibility – Trust	Completion (ending)
	Meaningfulness (values)

Table 1

The one Maslow meta-need that jumps into the foreground in the design of this book is *meaningfulness* a term easily seen as having interdependency with *mindfulness*. Something is meaningful when it is valued and relevant, and to be viewed in that manner it would also need to be understood within its specific context. Not doing so would be *mindless* which defeats the concept of meaningfulness as a practical objective. Questions for potential study interest might be: (a) How can we enlighten and empower people to proactively strive towards *human growth and development?* (b) When in life should we expect to experience a level of self-actualization that allows us to witness on the horizon our own opportunity *for self-transcendence?*

What Questions do People Often Ask?

Most of us try innumerable times through our lives to answer the following basic questions about ourselves and how we fit in with what our acquired knowledge and experience has given us to work. For many of us we discover that the answers are heavily influenced by situational factors at the time we ask. Chances are that throughout our lives we are on a journey of discovery, and while the questions don't change, the answers may change significantly.

Contrary to the view that some people espouse, our purpose and meaning is not pre-programmed into us before birth. While DNA and genes inherited through *nature* certainly set the stage for what and who we become, we do know that *nurture* has an immense effect during the whole time of our lives. Beginning in early childhood there are choices to be made even with the smallest amount of knowledge and experience. And certainly before we attain adulthood, the rights and responsibilities that result from both our own decision-making, and that contributed by others, encourages us to define ourselves and to draw maps for our life and career journeys – even if they prove to be only temporary and in need of periodic updating.

At the most fundamental level, research indicates that we humans report the need to discover the *Purpose* and the *Meaning* of our lives. We engage with others in answering a few fundamental life management questions:

1. What do I stand for? (*A sense of purpose*)

2. How do I fit in with what has come before? (*A sense of history*)

3. How am I related to other people/events/forces? (*A sense of order*)

4. What can I hope for as I take action? (*A sense of outcome*)

The difficulty some people experience with this list of questions is that they may be too broad a concept for us to understand at a more practical level. Also, even if we have a high level sense of our purpose or meaning, we have little of value because without a sense of history, order and outcome no action is intended – and knowledge without action is socially meaningless.

Initially it may be easier to identify specific day to day concerns for which finding answers will have a timely outcome – and a "to-do" aspect. Some examples in the "finding meaning" through understanding our personal needs or contemplating our occasional aspirations include:

1. "When will I discover *my true calling*, and begin to live a more

integrated and meaningful life?"

2. "How can I become *more knowledgeable and competent* in a rapidly changing and stressful world?"

3. "How can I manage my way through these *mid-life/career disappointments,* and have a second chance to succeed?"

4. "How can I make my *life a memorable e*vent, and become an example for those in the future?"

And, from a more introspective point of view, we could focus on exploring the *motivation* and *energy* needed to more fully understand human development. Exploration into these topics may be helpful:

1. Our interest in developing an *interdisciplinary pe*rspective on human relationships and events

2. Our need to achieve a sense of personal *integration* and *wholeness* in a *differentiated* world

3. Our aspiration for a life well-lived on a seemingly *mindful,* rather than *mindless* journey

4. Our understanding of the value of *critical thinking* and *authentic dialogue* in communicating more effectively with others

5. Our belief in the value of *human progress* beyond our own time and lives

Conclusion
This chapter proposes that all people benefit intellectually and emotionally from understanding the interplay when becoming attentive learners about themselves and others in situations they share in common. Subsequently, the leadership skills that evolve from this understanding can enable all involved to reason

holistically and mindfully when seeking answers to short-term situational problems and solutions -- as well as their personal contemplation concerning the overarching meaning of their lives.

The roles of female coach or women entrepreneur, in particular, are significant given (a) their gender which has a natural inclination towards the use of intuition, relationships and empathy when providing emotional support to others, and (b) their professional skills and leadership in conducting interviews, assisting clients in understanding their issues more clearly, and in choosing appropriate steps for issue resolution or service delivery.

About the Author

In his early public sector career Dr. Garrity was a manager, consultant, and educator with executive level experience in public and private sector organizations. In the U.S. Department of Defense, he was a professor of systems acquisition management at a defense college and a program/budget manager in a major Army command. For a U.S. intelligence agency he was the director of system acquisition management training, chairman of public sector management training, and a leader in quality management implementation.

Also, in the private sector Dr. Garrity was an executive consultant and project manager specializing in business development, process reengineering, quality management, organizational learning, e-business planning, knowledge management, acquisition program management, and organizational transformation. His formal education includes a BS, MBA, MPA and DPA.

Now in his semi-retirement career Dr. Garrity allocates his time between management consulting, educational course development and teaching in university human capital and public sector management programs. He is the founder of the nonprofit American Learnership Forum (ALF: www.alforum.org) and director of the ALF Center for Life Management and Professional Performance

Dr. Garrity has been trained and certified as an educational professional, authentic personal branding coach, and as a project management consultant. He is a published author who writes articles and presents conference briefings on a variety of topics directed toward personal fulfillment, organizational high performance, the community common good, societal enlightenment, mid-life transition, and senior rejuvenation.

His published books are Authentic Personal Branding (no longer in print), and available on Amazon.com are (1) An Introduction to American Learnership: Total Learning, Knowing and Leading as a Mindful Way-of-Being, and (2) the recently published Your Integral Life Matters: Create a Life and Legacy Management Mindset for Learning, Leading and Legacy Success – in the American Tradition.

Dr. Garrity's current focus is on establishing a national network of Integral Life and Legacy Management Affiliates for local area consulting and coaching. His 20 hour training webinar certification program can be freely reviewed at www.alforum.org for self-study (select the Read-Handbook tab). Rudy can be reached by phone at 703.587.0942 and at email rgarrity@alforum.org.

Female Entrepreneurship: Your Purpose, Your Passion, Your Coach
By Paul Garwood

To be successful as a female entrepreneur, your brand has to be your purpose and your passion. As a Life Empowerment and Career Coach I have helped female client's get a clear understanding of what a Purpose is and the connection to their brand, entrepreneurship, and bottom line. Utilizing a coach to help you determine if your brand is your purpose, leads to personal growth. It enables you to talk to someone that has walked the path you are attempting to walk. So now let's discover how working with a coach can help you grow, help you succeed, and help your bottom line.

THE MEANING OF PURPOSE

Life is a precious gift that we are given only once. However, the sad reality is that most of us don't value life the way we should. We are so caught in the monotony of the fast-paced life that we forget to find out the real meaning and purpose of life. As an entrepreneur it is a must that you realize what the real meaning and purpose of life is.

Most of the people I know either don't have a purpose in life or they think that there is no need to have a purpose. But I believe that unless you have a purpose in life, you won't be able to achieve self-actualization i.e. live a life that reflects your true potential or merit.

A life without a purpose is similar to a boat adrift is the sea with no telling what the final destination is.

The discovery itself that life must have a purpose represents a profound awakening that comes with the divine responsibility inherent in everyone that we must make our life meaningful not just ourselves but others around us – our loved ones and strangers alike.

But the question arises what is the real meaning of purpose? Why is there even a need to seek a purpose?

Let's look at the basic definition of purpose:
The reason for which something is done, or for which something exists.

When put in the context of life, the purpose takes a bigger meaning that encompasses the very essence of one's existence. You will find your life to be more meaningful when you know your true purpose in life.

Imagine for a moment a spoon that has a soul and consciousness. Days and months go by with the spoon remaining in the cupboard shelf. It feels uneasy inside, but does not know why. It feels that something is missing in life but does not know what it is.

Then someone pulls it out of the cupboard shelf and starts eating the cereal. The spoon feels a sense of extreme bliss and happiness being held and being used by another person for eating the cereal. At the end of the day, when the spoon is again placed inside the shelf, it feels like a transformed being – happy, fulfilled, and satisfied inside.

In short, the spoon has understood its real meaning or purpose in life. It has come to the realization what he was truly designed for and meant to do. Now it knows what its soul has been yearning for all along.

The purpose can be said to be one's destiny or a calling that once answered can take the person to the heights of success.

At the first glance, the purpose may seem to be a grand word that is best reserved for a gifted few. However, the reality is that we all have the capacity and ability to work for which we are made for. We all have the power, the potential and the ability to achieve great works by fulfilling the purpose in life.

All that is required is finding out the real purpose or destiny in life.

The truth is that most of us already know what our purpose or destiny is – it's lingering within us all the time. It's just that we are too scared (or too lazy) to claim it.

You need to stop making statements such as, "I've no clue what I should do with my life."

Instead, you should ask yourself what I could do to make life more meaningful for myself, and also others. As an entrepreneur this is a necessity.

Whenever you get up in the morning, if you don't feel enthusiastic or happy, then it's likely that you are not living your destiny or purpose in life. This is one of the major reasons individuals, women especially seek to become an entrepreneur.

In stark contrast, when you know the purpose (or you have unconsciously discovered the purpose) in life, you will feel fully rejuvenated and 'alive' in the morning. You will be eager to leave your bed every single day, and go to the destination come hell or high water.

That's the power of living a purposeful life; a life that you enjoy and through which you are able to make a meaningful impact on others.

Finding the purpose, in other words, refers to the sense of examining our strengths, weaknesses, and mental and physical resources, and then thinking about ways that they can be utilized to make a meaningful impact on not just our life, but also that of others.

The meaning naturally arises within us. No one can point to us what our purpose is, or what it should be. Only we have the power of realizing our true purpose.

When you strive to discover your purpose, you will own it and this will allow you to own your brand. And only once you own that brand will you be able to commit to your brand with all your heart and mind. For this, you need to tune into yourself and make an inward journey to discover your true self.

Through the self-discovery, you will be able to develop a full awareness of your own true nature as a human being. It will lead you to a heightened self-awareness that will ultimately result in leading a highly fulfilled and purposeful life.

Clarifying and finding out the real purpose in life will provide you with greater mental clarity as well. It will scatter the clouds of uncertainty hovering inside the mind, and make you better see the road that lies ahead.

5 Ways Finding Your Purpose Helps You as an Female Entrepreneur and Helps Your Bottom Line

1. Perform Actions that Align with your Goals of Entrepreneurship
When reading the book titled, E-Myth: Why Most Small Businesses Don't Work, I was deeply moved when I read the chapter where the author, Michael Gerber asked the readers to do a visualization exercise.

He instructed to visualize the day of our funeral. How you want yourself to be remembered? What should your eulogy consist of? Is it what you are doing right now?

After reading the chapter, I started listing the things that I felt are most important for me and which I would want others to remember about me. It was then that I realized that my current actions did not align with my personal values.

What I'm trying to say is that by having a purpose in life, your actions will be perfectly aligned with your values, your personal mission, and your goals. Every new day will bring you the opportunity to fulfill your heart's wishes.

If your current actions do not align with your values and beliefs, then I can guarantee you that you will not end your life on a peaceful and contented note, regardless of how much money you make or how much wealth you acquire.

2. Achieve Personal Excellence as an Entrepreneur

Finding the purpose in your life will allow you to achieve your personal excellence. Let's confess it; the main reason that you are reading this book is that you want to improve yourself as an entrepreneur. Otherwise, you might find it more entertaining to pass time watching a movie, playing a game, or reading a magazine containing celebrity gossip.

The fact is that the desire for personal excellence is innate in every one of us. Deep inside, every one of us wants to achieve personal growth. It's natural that you have the desire to being your best self and attain excellence.

As Aristotle had once famously stated: "Excellence is not an act, but a habit."

The habit to attain personal excellence can be attained by first seeking the purpose in life.

3. Live a Deeply Contended and Happy Life as an Entrepreneur

Having a purpose and attaching a meaning to life brings great inner joy and happiness. Regardless of whether you are busy creating a million goals and activities, you won't feel contended unless you have a clear purpose in life - a purpose that you believe in wholeheartedly.

You will never feel contented and at ease if your goals and actions have nothing to do with a higher purpose in life. One day you will come to the realization, 'Hey, that's not how I really wanted my life to be after all.'

The great management guru and self-help expert Stephen Covey said in his book, The 7 Habits of Highly Effective People, "If the ladder is not leaning against the right wall, every step that we take just gets us to the wrong place faster."

When you don't identify a purpose – a purpose that can stir your soul and shake your heart – you won't be able to live a happy life.

While having a purpose won't make all your problems disappear, it will certainly make you oblivious and immune to the life's problems, and as the great poet English Thomas Champion had once stated: "scorn all the cares that fate, or fortune brings."

4. Pursue Greater Goals
Without knowing your purpose in life, you won't be able to differentiate between important and unimportant goals. In fact, you will waste your life pursuing goals that won't make a meaningful impact on your inner well-being.

The tragedy of today is that most people blindly conform to the societies' vision of a happy life that ultimately does not bring any great joy in life. Earn more money > Buy a house / car > Buy another house /car > earn more …. Without a purpose in life, you will be inundated with the petty societal goals and then go to the grave with a heavy heart.

Having a purpose will allow you to cut through the societal crap and aim for the goals that truly matter to you, and which will fill your heart with joy and happiness.

When you find purpose in your life, you will be filled with so much energy and passion that you will continually look excited each day. Every day you will bound out of bed in a jovial mood and keyed up to do the things that you care the most. You will dread wasting hours as you would much rather pass time performing the work you love than passing time idly.

Having a purpose, in short, will provide you access to an unlimited source of energy. You can channelize the energy to achieve greater things in life. This is what many people say when they pursue their purpose. And the best thing is that they don't exhaust the energy even after working 10, 20, or 30 years doing the things that achieve a greater purpose.

On the other hand, if you don't have a purpose your life will feel like an empty vessel with no meaning. You will long for the weekends and dread the going to the office on Mondays. You will feel resistance in getting up every day going to work as it is not in tuned with your inner values.

If you find that you are looking forward to weekends and holidays as opposed to doing what you are doing each day, it's time that you find a purpose in life. It is a sign that you are not made to perform the task. It is an indication that something is seriously amiss in your life and you need to discover that missing link in order to live a fulfilled life.

5. Achieve Success (In Your Own Way!)

Most people, and especially entrepreneurs, focus too much on success. The general thinking is that success is an end goal in itself. However, I want to emphasize that success is entirely different. Real success should not be defined by societal norms or thinking.

Success, in fact, is doing the things that you really want to do, and excel in your task. It is the journey that you undertake while performing the activities that you love as compared to what others things that you should do.

When you have discovered your purpose in life, you will be doing exactly the things that bring joy and happiness.

Remember that you are the architect of your own life. No one owns you or can direct your life. Only you have the power and the right to define your life and success.

In conclusion, having a purpose in life acts life a fuel injector that allows you to drive through harsh terrains and successfully reach your destination of being a successful entrepreneur. Whether it takes one hour or 10,000 hours to achieve the goals, you will never be tired when you have a purpose or a goal in life and this will help you bottom line.

Instead of focusing on petty goals, you must discover your purpose in life and then create your goals around that purpose. It's more important that you first discover what you truly care for, make it your purpose, and then focus your energy on fulfilling what you feel is your purpose in life.

THE NEW YOU: A SUCCESSFUL FEMALE ENTREPRENEUR
Finding your purpose to be a Successful Female Entrepreneur will allow you to develop these 4 steps:

1. Increased Focus
Why you clearly know the purpose of your life, and perform the activities that will allow you to live a purposeful life, it will become allow you to focus more clearly on the matters that are important to you.

Many people find that this is the most valuable benefit of going through the entire process of finding a purpose. The purpose of your life will guide you in making the right decision about where to invest your efforts, money, time and talent.

When the life is without a purpose, you will feel confused and scattered like a boat adrift on the ocean with no destination. The purpose in a sense acts like a ship's rudder that will focus the ship in a single direction allowing you to reach the intended destination.

2. Experience Greater Self-Esteem
Having discovered a purpose and working to fulfill the same will encourage you to have a trust in your instinct, feelings, likes, dislikes, and thoughts. You will have more confidence in your own actions. This increased self-esteem will, in turn, propel you to achieve greater things in life.

When you work to fulfill a greater purpose, you esteem is not easily shattered by the views of others, or even by your own internal negative dialogue. You will focus on your skill, talents, and vision that will greatly strengthen your sense of self.

3. Instill Powerful Passion

Passion is a powerful emotion that once stirred can make you perform extraordinary feats. It is like a fuel to the fire that once ignited can take you to unchartered territories that you had never imaged before.

Living a life of purpose will make your life bright and lively. You will never be bored of the work and enjoy each moment of your life. Once you discover your purpose and work towards achieving the purpose in life, you will transform your brand from being black and white to a beautiful multicolored tapestry that is filled with passionate moments.

4. Tireless in Overcoming Obstacles

Having a purpose in life will allow you to become tireless in achieving your goals. The longer you remain true to your purpose, the more you will allow it to shape your life. Not one moment of your life will feel dull and tiring to you.

Whether your purpose is simply to spread a smile everywhere or as broad as ending poverty and hunger from the world, you will not see the task as an insurmountable mountain. Instead, you will see it as a small hill that you could easily overcome through patience, persistence, and hard work.

You will have a heartfelt sense of purpose that will bring joy and happiness in life. Your life will feel more meaningful and valuable to you. Every passing day will bring increased joy, increased pleasure, increased happiness, and an increased sense of satisfaction in life and this will power you and your brand.

About the Author

Paul Garwood is a Master Life Coach, Life Transition Expert, Life Empowerment Expert, Professional Speaker, Author and Radio Personality.

Paul is the Founder and President of Strive To Succeed Everyday and S2SE Life Coaching. S2SE is a Speaking, Coaching and Training Company that focuses on a number of topics:

1. Accountability
2. Goals
3. Leadership
4. Personal Development
5. Mentoring
6. Life Transitions
7. Life Empowerment
8. Parents of At-Risked Kids

S2SE works with individuals, families, teams and corporations to help improve accountability, effectiveness and efficiency seeks to empower by developing a positive mindset. Today there is much negativity flowing throughout World.

Strive To Succeed Everyday motivates and inspires their clients to never give up on themselves or their goals.

Author: "Finding Your Purpose: An Inspirational Guide To Re-Ignite Your Life's Purpose And To Live A Totally Content Life" or: "FINDING YOUR PURPOSE: AN INSPIRATIONAL GUIDE TO RE-IGNITE YOUR LIFE'S PURPOSE AND TO LIVE A TOTALLY CONTENT LIFE"

Paul is also the host of the Push Through w/Paul Garwood Radio Show which can be heard live on the Life enhancement Radio Station and also on iHeart radio and iTunes.

Paul is a sought after Coach, Expert and Speaker. If your need is for a dynamic coach, speaker, and expert to motivate, inspire and captivate you or your audience– look no further!

Paul resides Harper Woods, Michigan. In addition to building both Strive To Succeed Everyday and S2SE Life Coaching – Paul also enjoys spending time playing and coaching sports, reading, and exercising.

888-998-9961
plgwoodjr@strivetosucceedeveryday.com
www.strivetosucceedeveryday.com
www.s2selifecoaching.com

How Life Coaching Can Improve Your Bottom Line

By Denise Hansard

I wasn't sure I would make it ...

My youngest nephew, Ethan, and I took a trip to Peru in August of 2015. Our trip was to hike the Inca trail for 4 days ending our journey in Machu Picchu. Little did I realize how challenging this trip would turn out to be ... physically, mentally, and spiritually. Along with how this one experience, even now, has continuously given me inspiration and financial freedom in the world of being an entrepreneur.

Each day began hiking an average of 10 miles over a stony path, which was either basically up flights of stairs (literally) or down flights of stairs (literally) – all at a minimum of 10,000 feet above sea level. Sometimes, my stride was not long enough to traverse some of the rock stairs having to jump down or climb up being pulled by someone else. Imagine being on a Stairmaster for hours/miles at a time continuously setting a steady pace at the highest altitude you have ever been. Daunting, to say the least, and scary ... my fear of failing ran true in my head.

What I discovered about myself ...

Hiking for that length of time – not a problem. Climbing stairs, up and down – not a problem. Sleeping in a tent on a small pad for 3 nights – not a problem. Not showering for 4 days – my ultimate limit and yet not a problem. Being at an altitude of over 10,000 feet to 14,000 feet above sea level – this was the problem. I developed altitude sickness ... physical distress from difficulty adjusting to lower oxygen pressure at high altitude.

Our journey began with an overnight stay in Lima then traveling on to Cusco for two days. This was to acclimate us to the altitude of 11,000 feet above sea level. Trust me, two days were not enough. Touring around Cusco, catching our breath, as often as we could, was just the beginning of the challenge that was to be faced.

On the first day of the hike, we began with a bus ride to our starting point for the Inca trail. This day was to be the easiest day of the 4-day trek. Now Ethan, at 19, was not daunted by the trek. He was easily taking this trail of an upward climb with seemingly no problems. I, on the other hand, was finding some difficulty with all the stony stairs that our group was climbing. Easy, my foot! This was the thought going through my mind beginning to fear that my body would hold up.

Then day 2 of the hike began – the most difficult day. This day was to take our group to the highest point of our journey – 14,000 feet above sea level. The stony stairs become more difficult and seemed to have multiplied eliminating any smooth flat walking opportunities. This is when my altitude sickness kicked in. I became winded and nauseated with some light-headedness. Milagros, our guide, was there with me to keep me motivated and to make sure I didn't drop dead at any moment, I am sure. At one point, I literally didn't think I was going to make it. My fear grew with each step and laborious breath I struggled to take. I had hit a wall!

I know you have been there just as I was … maybe it was a personal wall or a professional wall. That time where you wondered how you were ever going to survive whatever new challenge you were experiencing personally or professionally.

From this experience, I learned three things that keep me going and I have used in my business.

1. **My commitment** – I had made a commitment to my nephew that we, together, would make this journey. With this commitment to him, I also made a commitment to myself to do this. This was foremost in my mind. If I gave up, then I would be disappointing him and myself. I don't give up! This is the same philosophy that I live by as I go about my

day to day activities for my business. When I made the decision to become a Life Architect and Speaker, I didn't give up. Especially when I have those moments of financial fear, imposter syndrome based upon fear, or fear of success in my business. All those wonderful fear moments knowing these are just moments and not my reality.

2. **Pushing myself past my comfort zone** – I was in pretty good shape. Yet, how do you train in Chicago for this type of change in altitude. I had no problem with going down or on steady inclines. My problem was with the upward (almost straight up at times) stairs that seemed as if they would never come to an end! I kept pushing myself by repeating in my head ... "slow and steady wins the race" along with "baby steps will get me up the mountain". Digging deep down inside myself with my mantra was the only thing that pushed me beyond my comfort zone and on to my goal.

   Ahhh, the comfort zone ... this is what I assist my clients on getting out of. I don't allow them to stay stuck in it. I wrote my book on this exact thing ... *Suffering in Comfort, How Owning Your Choices Will Set You Free*. What I know about that comfort zone ... this is your opportunity to grow. When you become anxious or fearful in a challenge that you want to succeed in, is the universe pushing you to grow, to do something different than you have ever done before, to get uncomfortable, fearful and do it anyway? Pushing beyond and succeeding!

3. **Accepting help** – Milagros, our wonderful guide, suggested that she carry my daypack for me. Now it was not extremely heavy, yet it would be one less weighted item for me to struggle with at this time of need. At first, I began refusing her help – normal for most people as we find it difficult to accept help much less ask for much it. Then I recognized that in order for me to survive this trek, I needed help and I needed to say 'yes' to the help that was offered. So, on the upward portions of the trail, I accepted that help. I didn't see

this as a failure, I saw it as a means to an end as my commitment to Ethan, and that took priority.

Knowing when to accept help or to even recognize when you need to ask for help is key to improving the bottom line in your business. When you find that you are exhausted in the daily activities of running a business ... the sales, the marketing, the finances, the administration, the coaching, the speaking ... this is when you bite the bullet and ask for help. This help can come in the form of hiring a virtual assistant or a coach, or a sales rep. You do this even when your fear is rearing its ugly head saying you can't afford it. What I am saying is that you can't afford not to ask, in order to move beyond your fear.

Fear Usually Stops Us — and How to Get Started Again

Fear will always be with you. That is the first thing you will need to admit to yourself. You can never be 'fearless'. Fear is that emotion that can be your foe or your friend. How to do you make it your friend? It's what you *do* with your fear that allows you to move out of your "stuckness". You choose to have fear push you forward instead of holding you back.

Opportunities come into your life every day. Someone may talk to you about a new job or a seminar she wants you to attend. Or you may have a chance to do something you truly love: start a business, have the wonderful relationship you are looking for, or move up that career ladder and make more money than you have ever have.

When these opportunities come, you have three choices:
- Say "yes" and step into your growth
- Say "no" and own this choice — even if you might regret it later
- Make no choice whatsoever, letting the opportunity pass you by — and then looking back and making excuses for why you didn't make a decision

In reality, there are really only *two* choices you can make: yes or no.

Allowing chances to slip away due to fear, lack of clarity, or just convincing yourself that you don't have the time, money or education is *not* a choice. It's just your fear getting in the way and blinding you to better outcomes.

Use ROAR to Tame your Fear

I have developed a four-step practice that will help you to tame your fear, called ROAR. A methodology to make fear your friend.

> **R – *Recognize*** that fear is just a state of being in your life at this moment—and that it will not last forever. Our bodies aren't physically able to maintain this highly charged emotional state for long. Once we recognize our fear and how it shows up for us, we can move to the next step.

> **O – *Open up*** to how your body has been conditioned to feel in fear. Are you feeling constricted, as though you're being choked or suffocated? Or just tired? Be open to these feelings and to the possibility of choosing to feel differently. You can decide to no longer view it as debilitating and limiting— choose to see and feel it as more powerful and enriching— because this is an opportunity for you.

> **A – *Accept*** the new feeling that you now associate with fear. Fear is just that: an opportunity to step out of what we know now and into the unknown where beautiful things can happen. Breathe into this newness of growth, allowing your mind to catch up with your feelings. Own it and make it yours.

The last step is really a two-fold step:

> **R – *Release*** your old feelings, your old fear story and **Replace** it with the new one. When you begin to feel the old story surfacing, immediately stop whatever it is that you are doing; literally hit your internal pause button. Say out loud or to yourself, "This is no longer me. I choose to move out of my comfort into something *more*."

This practice of **ROAR** is commonly called a "pattern-interrupt process": a behavioral shift. We begin to notice the pattern that has been our story for so long and literally choose a different one.

Our thoughts, our memories and our stories have an attachment to us — our stories become our memories. Good and bad memories latch on to us as muscle memory. We tend to only remember the bad (failures) muscle memories, including those created by fearful moments in our lives. Whatever story you have had in the past has literally become part of your body and have made you who you are. This then creates your thoughts. When you begin to recognize your thoughts as these thoughts are happening, you have the power to ask, "Is it really me?"

Our thoughts create our reality

Wallace Wattles, an American Author and New Thought writer, is best known for a 1910 book called *The Science of Getting Rich* in which he explained how to become wealthy. I have this book and have read it many times. I even did an experiment with this book in which I read and studied only 4 chapters of this book for 90 days straight. It took me over 6 months to do this, as there was a day that I completely forgot about my experiment of studying and absorbing the essence of this book thus having me start over from day 1 - discipline.

What I love about this book is how he explains the process of our thoughts. The process of how our thoughts (becoming our beliefs) can create whatever it is we truly desire in life … if we make it a part of us and take action.

Mr. Wattles states: "Thought is the only thing that can produce tangible riches … Man is a thinking center, and can originate thought. All the forms that Man fashions with his hands must first exist in his thoughts; he cannot shape a thing until he has thought that thing."

Basically, what he is saying is that everything is created twice ... first in our thoughts and then in reality. The home you designed ... first it was a thought. The invention of the combustible engine was first a thought. If you can imagine it in your mind, then there is a way to create it. The way to do this is to believe in you and that you can take actions steps to create it.

We do this type of creation all the time without even realizing that we are doing it. We proclaim how bad we feel even when initially we weren't feeling bad then someone says we look like we don't feel well. We live from a place of scarcity when we continually claim that we "can't afford" even the smallest things of pleasure. We have to save for that "rainy" day holding on tightly to everything that we have. When we do this, we begin the process of "choking" other opportunities out of our life.

The most common way of "creating from our thoughts" is through our choices of how we talk – internally to ourselves and externally to others. How often do you find yourself saying these common phrases ...?

> *"I can't"*
> *"I don't know"*
> *"I'm sorry"*
> *"I wish I could"*
> *"Let me ask/check ..."*

All of these phrases give away your power --- allowing you to not be responsible to you and your beliefs. These words are harsh and I believe in the power of our thoughts creating our reality.

What if you changed your words to make them more empowering and more positive? Instead of saying "I can't", say "I choose"; "I don't know" say "Let me find out or tell me more"; "I'm sorry" say "I feel for your pain or I understand".

Saying things like "I wish I could" or "Let me ask/check ..." is basically saying that you have no power to make a decision. Why not claim your power back and say "I am working on achieving that"? These are my words. You have your own way of reframing these phrases to make them more empowering. Choose the empowering words instead of the disempowering words.

Our thoughts come from the conversation we are telling ourselves ... can't do it, not good enough, what makes me think I can this time ... all these conversations are a choice we make to keep us stuck in our pain. I can relate as I was there once. What choices are you making? Choices of conversation that can keep you stuck in pain or empowered to move forward? Only you can choose and you don't have to do it alone.

A pain, a hurt, a loneliness ... these are all parts of our stories from our past. But we also have memories of successes: getting the "A" on a test when you didn't think it was possible or winning an award or million-dollar project. Remembering the successes in your life — this muscle memory of *success* from your past — is what you need to put *first* in your being. You must invite these success memories to replace the less empowering thoughts: the memory of failure.

We *have* our story, but we *are not* our story. We have our memories, but we are not our memories.

You now have the basics for "Taming your Fears through ROAR" along with how your thoughts create your life. Put these tools of behavioral change into practice. Allow fear to become your friend through this process and not continue to be your foe, keeping you stuck in the comfort zone of pain. Change your words to empower yourself for abundance.

What do you want?

Every one of us has a purpose. Every one of us is here for a reason. Your job is probably OK - yet you feel as if you have been pigeon holed, undervalued and always being overlooked for that next promotion. Your relationship is OK - yet you want more passion, spontaneity, more of what it used to be when you first fell in love. Your health is OK - yet it is easy to turn off the alarm on your phone - saying you will go to exercise class tomorrow morning.

How do you go from playing small in your life to living your life to the fullest?

Playing small is another way of fear showing up in your life. We have already learned the ROAR process. Now, let's move on CLEAR ... a process to show you how to transform your life – into the life you were meant to live to be abundant in your life and business.

CLEAR – 5 steps to transforming your life

> **C – Choice**: Recognize that everything in life is a choice. Every thought you have, every action you take, every involuntary reaction you make is a choice. You have become conditioned to think that sometimes You don't have choices. That, in and of itself, is a choice — to be in a victim state of being. Everything in life is a choice, and you make it.

> **L – Language**: How we express our thoughts in spoken words comes from your choices. You learn patterns of language that keep you victimized or help you to grow into victors! A good example of this is the use of the word "but." This is overused and has become a filler word in our language. Yet, its meaning is extremely powerful. Everything you state *after* this word negates everything you said *before* it! Example: "I love you **but** I don't like what you did." The first part — stating you love someone — is totally wiped away with that three-letter word: but. This one word stops most of us from living our life to the fullest, as we allow it to put the brakes on what we really want. My best advice is to get rid of the word altogether! Instead of having it as a filler word, put a period at the end and start a new sentence. Example: "I love you. I don't like what you did." This totally changes the emotions behind what is being said. Use positive language in everything you say.

> **E – Energized**: When you make your words positive, those words will energize you to begin the process toward change,

toward transformation. We just looked at how our words have power. Our words can change relationships with ourselves and with others. Remember: what we say to ourselves (internal trash talk: "I can't," "what makes me think it will work this time," etc.) is usually how we live our life. This always moves us in the direction of "not good enough" behaviors. Energize your words into positive ones. This one step will create change for the better.

A – Actions: We take action from a different perspective based upon the power of our words. Energize your words by making them positive: "why not" instead of "why"; "I choose" instead of "I can't"; "I am" instead of "I want, hope, wish." This allows you to take action steps with more confidence and assurance, rather than from a place of uncertainty, doubt and despair. Claim your power!

R – Results: Your results become more attuned to the idea to "live like you were meant to." When you make defined choices, your life flows with ease. There is less stress because you are choosing the *results* and not allowing *circumstances* to rule your life.

If you don't like the results in your life, then go back to your choices. Your choices can change your life! I know as I have made those choices to change my life.

Inca Trail and the end ...

The last two days of trekking were not as bad as the first two. I got better and soon began to carry my own weight, so to speak. This was the greatest physical challenge that I faced in my life. There have been many other emotional challenges that I have faced and have forged through. It was only with having had those emotional challenges in the past that helped me to make this very challenging physical journey.

So, now, when I face a daunting task in my professional life – where will my next client come from, what steps do I take to continue my revenue growth, how to not allow disappointments and rejection keep me down, etc. – I know I have what it takes to make the journey. I just remember my mantras and the success of having reached the pinnacle of the mountain. I don't allow my fear or my lack of clarity to stop me. I keep moving past my limited thinking and my fear. I remember the clearness of my why, because that is what it takes. It is with all of this that my business soars and continues to grow. It can be the same for you when you decide to step into more. More of the confidence to take those risks and grow your business. More of the clarity in knowing what your next steps are going to be without second-guessing. *More of you being you ... authentic & loving life!*

Since I started my coaching business 6 years ago, I have always had a coach of some type ... media, business, pricing, retreat ... what I needed at each moment to grow myself and my business. What I can say is that the one type of coach that was most beneficial was my life coach. It was with her that I was able to own my stories of the past to move beyond those stories. It was with these insights that I began the journey of empowerment to move beyond my fear and my feeling of "not good enough." It was with my life coach that I stepped into greatness. I would not be the successful abundant coach that I am today without my life coach. That is what a great life coach can do for you ... move you out of what has kept you stuck in your life to what can be your greatest self.

My advice to anyone looking to move up the career ladder, start your own business, or seek out that new relationship, is to work with a life coach first, before any other coach. This is the best gift you can give yourself. Doing this will have you make a quantum leap in any endeavor you step in to as you will have already done the hard part, learn about your behaviors that are keeping you stuck, and know the steps needed to move forward with love for yourself in all that you do to become your best self! Find that type of life coach and you will go far!

On the last day of our trip together, Ethan posed one question to me ... *"Is Mt. Kilimanjaro our next adventure."* He has a great sense of humor!

3 things to know about Denise Hansard, Life Architect

1. ***Didn't just hang her shingle out as a coach*** ... Masters in Counseling (working therapeutically & in the personal development growth arena), Certified Pricing Professional (those 20+ years in the corporate world teaching the art, science and value of pricing ... your worth in it), Life Coaching Certification (getting back to her gift as a Life Architect, helping women design their one life from the inside out)

2. ***Been there, done that*** ... successfully started 2 businesses & climbed the corporate ladder, lived to tell about it all always fully supporting herself financially, and never looked back. Have coached hundreds of women to generate 6 figure incomes, find the love of their life & take back their power. Have spoken on stages to groups of 5 to over 300 ... transforming the minds and hearts of CEOs, Executive Sales, Sales Teams, and anyone who would listen.

3. ***G.R.I.T.S*** ... Girl Raised in the South and owning every bit of that label. Knowing exactly who she is, what she brings to the table coming from the heart ... pushing clients to do and be more ... to take action in spite of every 'mean girl' thought and story they have.

About the Author

Denise Hansard is the author of *Suffering in Comfort* and is known around the world as an expert in transformation. She gives you the framework to better understand you (and your choices creating you), embrace who you truly are, and navigate your life (personally & professionally) as your authentic self with ease and grace as you only have one life. Through retreats, private and group coaching and speaking, Denise has changed lives. With her Masters in counseling, Pricing expert training and a certification in Life Coaching, she has coached hundreds of women to make 6 figures, find the love of their life and get super healthy.

C.H.A.N.G.E ... It's time for Change ... a 5-step process

You say ... Why Change?
I say ... Why Not Change?
Saying yes to change is the 1st step to the journey of becoming more YOU ... a more abundant attractor, a more empowered leader in your career, a more beautiful you inside and out!

Sign up below to receive my ebook on CHANGE absolutely free. It will assist you in accepting change as a welcomed friend and not as a hazard sign in life.

http://denisehansard.com/project/its-time-for-change/

HOW TO CONTACT DENISE:

Email: denise@denisehansard.com
Phone: 847-485-8446
Website: http://denisehansard.com

Confusing Your Self-Worth With Your Net Worth

By Jeannette Koczela

If you are a female entrepreneur, you have probably experienced the challenge of doubting your own ability--wondering if you're really capable of providing enough value to your clients/customers. So common is this experience that there are names for it. My coach calls it the "Imposter/Inferiority syndrome" where you look at your numbers, i.e. sales, subscribers, up-sales, etc., and equate the business's level of success or worth with your own value or worth. That makes you feel like an imposter, fraudulently taking people's money.

As women, we tend to over-deliver to our customers to make sure they feel good about us and perhaps, also unconsciously compensating for the imposter syndrome. This is a plight of the entrepreneur coupled with the plight of being a female with an innate tendency to nurture and care for our people, making sure everyone is happy.

Here's an example of how this imposter syndrome came up for me: The week started out great. I was in a good mood, and everything seemed to go well--and even when it didn't, it didn't bother me, because I was just enjoying my business and the running of it. But then, due to some unexpected setbacks towards the end of the week, doubt crept in like a fog, and by the end of the week, looking at my sales numbers, I started to question whether I was really providing enough value for what I was charging my clients.

This sort of doubt can lead to questioning your self-worth, and, if you let it persist, it will sabotage your business. You have a setback, feel bad about yourself, and then justify your negativity by looking at your numbers---low sales, your network is not growing as you'd like, your conversion rates are down, etc. Then that continues in a downward spiral of self doubt. The problem lies in confusing your self-worth with your net worth.

In my case, I knew I needed to get some support but I wasn't sure where to find it. I didn't want to upset my husband or any of my friends, for that matter. There were colleagues, but most of my colleagues that I was close to, were also clients, and my ego just didn't allow for me to be that vulnerable to clients. Sounds like a dead-end, right? Well, not exactly.

There was one source of inspiration and support, and that was in the skills I had learned from some of my past coaches. One technique I had learned was to ask for inner guidance on the issue. I did that, and some interesting things occurred. I'll tell you what happened and how you can use what I used to reclaim my self-worth for you.

1) Listing Accomplishments

The first thing that happened was that when I pulled out the homework assignment from a coaching program I was taking, it was to write out 101 of your lifetime accomplishments. I started writing and, as I wrote, I began to realize the magnitude of my true value.

As I listed my accomplishments, I realized that my value didn't have to be measured by my business successes or failures.

Sometimes as entrepreneurs, we get so caught up in the daily "grind" that we forget about what we've accomplished along the way. Doing an exercise like this is a great technique for overcoming negativity and reclaiming your own value because it forces you to review not only your business accomplishments but also your personal ones.

2) Using Broader Metrics

The second thing that happened was that night when I went to bed and started reading a book about entrepreneurship. It was discussing the concept of self-worth versus net worth. (Funny how books can just **happen** to address the conflict you are facing in the moment!) The author was saying that sometimes we entrepreneurs confuse our self-worth with our business net worth. And this presents a problem, because the two are not comparable. "Wow" I thought, "This is what I need to hear!"

In her book, "Killing It: An Entrepreneur's Guide to Keeping Your Head Without Losing Your Heart," Sheryl O'Loughlin says,

"If we think about our business in a more holistic sense, everything we do has positive impacts. And we need to learn to value those positive impacts that are outside of most traditional metrics. Then we will understand that there is more to business than traditional metrics of profit/loss."

As business owners, we are used to traditional metrics to measure how well we're doing in our business. Traditional metrics are profit-and-loss, sales conversions, and other financial numbers. But, as Sheryl points out, there are metrics apart from net worth that we should be taking into consideration.

For even if you separate self-worth from net worth, they still affect each other, and that's why it's important to broaden the metrics you are using.

Those other metrics include things like what kind of impact are you having on your clients lives, what kind of impact are you having locally and globally, and what is the legacy you are leaving.

Nowadays there are more and more business owners who measure their success based on their "footprint", such as how they are changing people's lives for the better, or how much are they not polluting the environment. (Notice that this does not include money or financial gain.)

Sheryl predicts: *"In ten years, there will be less room for companies that don't think about metrics other than financial ones."*

So another great exercise to do when you're **not** in a negative funk (and before you get into another one) is to write down — for future reference--what kinds of metrics you have accomplished with your business, other than financial.

For instance what kind of impact are you having on your clients lives? Are you making them happier? Are you improving their relationships with others? Are you giving them hope? Are you providing them with strategies that will make their business grow?

3) Documenting Your Value

Sheryl says, *"Tap into the values that are important to you. What is the greater purpose in your work beyond just a monetary one? Having this bigger picture helps you feel good about what you're doing beyond the ups and downs of business. It keeps your life aligned with your values, and helps you course-correct when you feel out of line. Having a greater purpose with your business reminds you that you're a valuable person in spite of numbers."*

When we question our own value, many times it's because we relate it to the value that we think we are or aren't giving our customers or clients. But nothing could be further than the truth. This concept of separating self-worth from net worth inspired me to realize that my value is always there, and I just have to make sure that I'm sharing it with my clients.

Another exercise that will help you understand your value is to write out a mission statement for your business. What is the big picture? Why is this important to you? How does it align with your personal values?

Answering these questions and writing out your mission for your business also keeps you in alignment when you encounter business challenges. Those challenges can make you wonder why you are doing this business, and your mission statement will remind you of the bigger picture and motivate you to persevere.

Reading Sheryl's book that night helped me gain a better understanding of the concept that I am a valuable person regardless of how my business is doing, and that got me out of my negative funk.

4) Getting Outside Support

Remember: your **own** worth is what you bring to the table. And it doesn't change. Your **net** worth can and will change. If you don't confuse the two, you can ride out any business challenge. But it's not easy to do this on your own. That's where a life coach can help. By being an objective observer and seeing the big picture, a coach can show you where your value is and help keep you in touch with it.

A coach can help you figure out what your purpose is and make sure your business purpose aligns with your personal mission and your values. And a coach can help you determine what kind of impact you are having on your clients' lives. Everyone needs a coach. Even 7-figure coaches have coaches.

In summary, I want to encourage you to use the following action steps (that I used) to stop yourself from entangling your self-worth with your net worth, which could be sabotaging your business:

1) Start a list of the 101 accomplishments of your lifetime. It may take you more than an hour or even several days to complete, and it can be an ongoing list.
2) Start another ongoing list of what kind of the positive impacts your business is having.
3) Write out a mission statement for your business.
4) Always have a coach you can turn to for support.

About the Author

Jeannette Koczela spent several decades as an Impressionist oil painter and working as a free-lance artist. Her interest in computers led her to become a graphic and web designer, and to create online products including a flash card set, a home study course, digital ebooks, and her first published book, "Money Mindset Makeover."

Then she discovered life coaching and went through certified spiritual life coach training. While coaching life coaches, she began to see a need for more ways for them to be seen online and connect with potential clients, and a way to learn more business skills. The idea of founding an association culminated in creating the "International Association of Professional Life Coaches®." The association offers an online directory, monthly Masterclasses, opportunities for publishing and speaking, through more visibility, credibility, and connection, and other business resources for life coaches.

Her second book, "Life Coach Business Blueprint" combined all the business and marketing skills she learned while running her own coaching business, and teaches new coaches how to run and market a coaching business.

Her third book, "The 7 Essential Steps to Get More Clients," answers 7 of the biggest questions coaches have about marketing with plenty of strategies and resources.

To get a free Life Coach Business Toolkit visit: www.iaplifecoaches.org/tools

To get her free ebook, *"7 Quick-Start Marketing Strategies to Get Clients This Week"* visit: www.jeannettekoczela.com

Email: jeannettekoczela@iaplifecoaches.org

Protect Your Day/ Protect Your Future
By Rick McLeod

Don't let your future be stolen one hour at a time.
Congratulations, you're a business owner. It doesn't matter if you are working part-time from home, or you are in a bright shiny new office space. It doesn't matter if you can put in 2-3 hours a day or you can commit to it full time. You are now a target. You will meet salespeople, hear from telemarketers, have friends and acquaintances drop by, family drop-in; and they all want the same thing, a piece of your time. Your time, in reality, is your money. Your money, in this case, is your future. So all these people are trying to steal your future.

In fairness, we have to say that the salespeople and telemarketers are professionals trying to do a job, and we have to remember they are accustomed to hearing no. So learn to say no, and learn to say it early in the communications. Not only are you saving yourself time and money, but also you are letting them get on with their job in finding someone who can use their service or product. The more time you give them, the more they have invested in converting you to a sale, and the more persistent they will be in following up and taking even more of your time.

Great. Now that we've recognized that your time is your future and how important it is to protect it, lets get down to the how's.

Boundaries
Let's assume for a moment that you have a spouse/partner. You did discuss with them that work time is work time. No? Then don't be surprised when you have unexpected social engagements, get the kids dropped off for you to watch, or have your spouse/partner drop by to visit because they're lonely or bored. Get it clear from the start and save a lot of headaches as you try to meet a deadline with "surprise company" coming by in fifteen minutes. This

arrangement applies equally to your home office as well as your regular office. Remember to be fair, though. If you have a deadline and have to work outside of your agreed upon hours, let them know.

Friends and relatives need to have the same understanding as well. Your business is not some little thing you are trying out for a few extra bucks on the side. It's a serious business, and you have to treat it as such. And so do friends and relatives. How you educate them as you start your business will have a lot to do with how successful you are. Just like a retailer, you have to have set hours.

When you have a job, you can't take personal calls at work that last twenty minutes plus, and you can't allow it in your business either. You are not going to break their habits instantly, but you have to be persistent and firm. "Sorry I'm up against a deadline, and I really can't talk right now, can I call you back? What's best for you, tonight at six or tomorrow morning?" It's a good idea always to give them two options. One, it lets them know you're not just blowing them off. Two, it shows that their time is important to you and you are making arrangements to fit into their schedule. Hopefully, this rubs off, and they return the courtesy.

The hardest to deal with are your children, especially the younger ones. They just don't understand why they can't go to Mommy with every little discovery, complaint or question like they always have before. They need to feel a real connection to the process. So, explain what you are doing and why, in a way that they will understand. Explain the benefit to them. And to make them feel a part of the process, have them work out the reward they will earn for letting you work. Make sure they understand that other parents work away from home and their children can't keep running to them during work hours.

Depending on the age of the child you can set short-term goals using, say, stars or stickers. E.g.: Say you work 4 days a week for 3 hours each time. Each time you work uninterrupted for 3 hours, they get a star. If they get three stars/stickers during a specific week you will take them for a treat. Note: the treat could be a trip to their favorite park, or you'll go biking with them, not necessarily taking them for ice-cream.

Distractions

One of the greatest causes of losing time at work can be your work area. A work area filled with piles of unfinished files, half-finished projects, your phone, iPad, computer, and other clutter is an invitation to flitter about from one thing to another and lose a day, not accomplishing a thing. You say you are great at multitasking? I think you should compare how many projects you complete by multitask vs. single focus projects that you do one after another over a set period. The research will show that you take from twenty-eight to forty plus minutes to completely refocus after being distracted. You can see what happens in a four hour work period with only a handful of events pulling your attention from what you had planned for your workday.

The answer is to de-clutter--not only your desk, but your whole work area. All projects should have separate files, if you require paper resources, and all files/resources should be off the desk or work area unless they pertain to the task at hand. You'd be surprised by how often just noticing a file out of the corner of your eye will draw your mind to it. Then you are making notes on it, you know, just taking a moment, but completely removing your attention away from the task at hand and requiring you to rebuild and refresh your concentration just to get back to where you were before you mentally wandered off. (Remember that 28+ minutes to refocus?)

Social Media

Turn it off. *I need it for my business.* Turn it off. *I'm only going to check my email.* Turn it off. I could keep going, but you get the picture. One quick check of your email can lead to seeing what's happening on Facebook or Twitter etc. and then you look up and discover your quick check of email has cost you over an hour. If you are working forty-five-minute or hour-long blocks and taking a break before starting another time block, you can use your break time to check your email, etc. Just don't be somewhere comfortable while you do it. Stand up, go outside, walk around--whatever it takes to keep you from drifting down the social media highway to nowhere.

Another thing you can do is to set a timer to control your time for email etc. Some like to do it first thing. Others prefer to accomplish some work on their major task for the day before opening their email. Replying to email can take up significant portions of your day. Remember, once you get in there, you are probably working on the "urgent to somebody else, but not so important to you" tasks. So, by the end of the day, you can be left feeling you've not accomplished anything towards what you wanted to accomplish, and you are no closer to your dreams.

Habits and Rituals
Shortly after I get up and start each day, I make my first cup of coffee. After stretching, I sit down with it to read from three daily positive daily thought books, have a short meditation session and review my affirmations. My daily ritual is not negotiable. I don't have to think about it. I just do it. The early morning time is my time and helps me set a positive framework for the day. My ritual works for me, but maybe not for you. You need to create a ritual that is your own, takes into account your situation, and has personal meaning for you, for example, getting kids ready for school.

Rituals are all about simplifying your life. They are something done as a normal protocol and, hopefully, will become a habit. You can have all kinds of rituals. One for waking up as illustrated above, one for starting work, one for ending the work day, or one for getting ready for bed. You can even have rituals about your clothing such as President Obama, or Steve Jobs had. (Although you may get tired of the same outfit day after day.) Because they are routine, rituals reduce the number of choices you have to make every day. They simplify life and help you leave mental space for the more important decisions of the day.

When you stop and think that we are bombarded by some thirty-five thousand- plus messages a day, you can see how easy it would be to become a victim of decision overload. The more decisions you have to make, the harder it is to make a decision. Nobody wants to be the person at the head of the line at the cashier trying to decide on buying the red foil wrapped chocolate or the green foil wrapped chocolate. <u>We</u> know it doesn't matter, but they just can't choose. (One of the easily observable reasons why rituals are so important.)

The next idea may seem to be unnecessary, but write down your rituals and refer to your list as you go through them. Especially when starting out, you might be surprised, like I was, by how often you miss one or more items if you are in a hurry that morning.

Lists

One of the greatest—but most poorly used--aids to planning is having a list of what you need to accomplish. I like the idea of having one list of work-related projects and another for everything else.

Some suggest that having a list for every separate topic is the way to go, but I found I could never find the list that I wanted when I needed it. I find that having just two lists works very well for me.

The Business List

Includes anything to do with your work itself. Does not include getting a new lunch bag or new clothing for work, but would include office supplies. Since each business is different, we'll picture a generic list that could include: who you need to meet with to work on different projects, projects in progress or upcoming, seminars or training you are scheduled to attend, and correspondence, etc.

The Other List

The other list will have everything else. Why bring up the other list in a business book? Because if it's not on a list, it's in the back of your mind, and things will pop up while you are working and can frequently distract you.

Referring back to assisting our ability to focus, this list will contain all those little things we need to do but keep in the back of our mind, and remember just after they were due, like remembering to pick up milk as you pull into your driveway.

A great way to build this list is to grab a notepad and start putting things down. If you have a house, go outside and look for things that you've meant to do like pull up the summer flowers or prepare to plant in the spring. Clean the gutters. Sweep the driveway, and so on. List any building projects you may have in mind for the future.

Then go inside and go to every room, listing anything you need to do. Repeat for each room on every floor.

Things not to forget:
Do you need to organize your CDs, DVDs, your Library? Do you have a collection or hobby area that you need to organize? What about your workshop? How is your closet? Do you have a lot of clothing that is too big or too small? If it's too big, get rid of it. The thought of having to replace it will help you maintain your weight. If it's too small, get rid of it. When you lose weight, treat your self to a new wardrobe. (Shopping might be a great incentive for some.) Either way, you have rid yourself of a lot of closet space and cleared clutter from your shelves.

Once you have this big list, you can rearrange it, making sub-sections such as: "cleaning", "decluttering", "maintenance and repair", "shopping for furniture", and "supplies". You can also have sections for "vacations I'd like to take". The list can and should contain fun activities that you want to make sure you don't forget.

The big thing to remember is to have a list that contains all these items, which you refer to weekly (or more often if required). This takes all these things out of your head and puts them somewhere they can be found and scheduled. Will all these things get done in a week or month? No. The idea is to be able to select what is important and leave the little things to fit into your schedule as filler, and not have the idea of picking up light bulbs push out the need to get your engine light checked. Unfortunately, we sometimes let the daily trivia overwhelm our schedule and leave us with our important tasks unfinished.

Action Steps

Set boundaries with spouse, children, friends, and family.

Clear your desk.

Clear your work area.

Turn off social media, and email if when appropriate.

Start to ritualize as much of the day as you can.

Make a business list.

Make the other list.

Segment your list.

Relax, it's going to be fine.

About the Author

Rick McLeod is the Director at I.R.M. Coaching Associates.

Rick has traveled an interesting path to becoming a Life Coach. Starting as a Guitar Instructor while still in high school, he went on to work for an international musical instrument company where he wrote songs for method books, articles for the teacher's newsletter, and taught at the national music camp and as a guest clinician at teacher seminars. He later worked in the Dealer Development area where he was Editor and wrote for the Company News Magazine.

Rick returned to teaching in London and also had a brief stint, writing, producing and even doing some photography on a video.
After studying Martial Arts for ten years, Rick opened a school. While teaching, he continued studying and is currently working on his Fifth Degree Black Belt. Unfortunately, due to a knee injury, he had to stop teaching.

After receiving his licenses for Insurance and Mutual Funds, Rick became a Financial Planner. Learning how poorly most people plan their finances, Rick became even more interested in life planning and coaching, after all, if something as important as finances were being left almost to chance by so many people, what about other areas of their lives.

One of Rick's key interests is in improving focus and time management systems. You'll see it on his web page. "Discover the power of Black Belt Focus." As well as hearing about it on his frequent radio guest spots.

"I help people learn and develop skills to tame their schedules and commitments so they can achieve more and have the time to appreciate the small things in life again."

Fill in the contact information on the website to arrange an introductory session.

www.irmcoachingassociates.com
rick@irmcoachingassociates.com

The Three R's For Female Entrepreneurs
By Ragini Michaels

Ever feel hesitant to declare yourself an entrepreneur? I wouldn't come near the notion for many years. Too scary and ripe with responsibilities I didn't want to touch – like gain and loss, and the bottom line!

But after 4 decades of undeniable success, it was just silly not to embrace the title. This is important. Not declaring your female entrepreneurial status to yourself and others makes it that much harder to understand and manage the unique stress and challenges that go with it.

Over those 4 decades I'm grateful to have discovered a few keys that make professional success and personal happiness an easier and less stressful challenge for women.

We do have a particular challenge that men just don't have. And that's what I want to share with you in this chapter.

We Are Caretakers Of The Heart

First, let's acknowledge that putting others first is baked into us. Women seem to be universally designed to care for others. Whether it's our estrogen or our culture, we usually don't even consider it a decision. We just do it. This is one of our defining and differentiating characteristics. I'm going to call it the Unconditional Motherly Love gene.

In the past years, we began entering the business world in more powerful and challenging ways. This shift hooked up the Unconditional Motherly Love gene to the Super Woman gene.

This caused the emergence of a powerful push-pull dilemma for every female entrepreneur. This generated quite a cast of new considerations and conundrums. And these consistently play a powerful role in creating our successes (and failures) as solo entrepreneurs.

Here's our unique push/pull:

> *EITHER be a wonderful, giving, loving woman demonstrating the power of unconditional love*
> *OR be a powerful, no holds barred, and cutting-edge leader capable of succeeding in a male dominated business world.*

It somehow slipped into our consciousness as an EITHER/OR proposition. And that means it exerts a powerful influence on our decision making process, and ultimately, our financial success. There's more on that later.

It seems our beautiful feminine trait of caring without concern for ourselves also contributes to many of our painful and frustrating business failures.

I was puzzled by how something so intrinsic to the female nature (caring about others and putting them first) could also be one of the biggest contributors to my frequently falling flat on my professional and financial face!

These turned out to be things like:
- ♥ Not being comfortable setting good boundaries
- ♥ Not being able to say no or turn someone away
- ♥ Not asking for the fee appropriate to my skill level
- ♥ Letting my heart take the lead, against my better judgment
- ♥ Making decisions that pushed the limits of my energy & time

As a Life Coach and Behavioral Change Specialist, I've coached many women who were frustrated and unhappy with their businesses and their lives. And they couldn't quite put their finger on what was happening.

Working with so many women over the years made it obvious that female entrepreneurs have to address a fundamental challenge unique to them.

Whether you have a partner and kids, are a single Mom, or have taken the path less traveled and remained unmarried and on your own, this challenge remains consistent.

Balancing The Super Woman Gene & The Unconditional Motherly Love Gene

Let me reiterate the unique challenge again:

EITHER be a wonderful, giving, loving woman demonstrating the power of unconditional love
OR be a powerful, no holds barred, and cutting-edge leader capable of succeeding in a male dominated business world.

Bottom line: no matter your circumstance, every female entrepreneur has this challenge:
EITHER I to attend to my own needs
OR I attend to the needs of others.

It makes no difference whether the 'other' is family, friends, clients, or the details of creating and maintaining your entrepreneurial enterprise. And curiously, the stress generated by this dilemma is often behind those financial decisions that don't turn out so well.

The Super Woman gene divides your workload between business and family/friends. You have to attend to both as the Super Woman gene demands. But you can only handle one of them at a time. This is why the scenario is so deeply distressing. Which do you choose?

You find yourself of 2 minds about the answer. On one hand, you have to take care of your business. But while you're doing it, you fear your relationships will suffer. On the other hand, you have to take care of your family and friends. But while you're doing that, you fear your business and financial commitments will suffer.

The real issue here is that an entire category of concern doesn't even reach the agenda. The Super Woman gene completely leaves YOU out of the picture and will demand you take up no room in the daily calendar.

Let's take a look at what I mean.

What We Unconsciously Expect Of Ourselves
I think you'll agree that the demands emerging from each of the following four categories eats up a huge portion of your daily energy, attention, and focus. With the Super Woman gene in operation, we don't even question the reasonableness of assuming so many conflicting pressures.

- **The Outer Face Of Your Business**: Making sure you put your client's interests over your own. That fundamental decision puts everything flowing in the right direction for both efficiency and effectiveness. It's the bottom line - hence, the name of my own business. If you can do this, success will almost certainly knock on your door. But if you don't do it properly, you'll end up making your life about your clients, booking meetups and talking with clients without regard for your own personal time separate from work.

- **The Inner Face Of Your Business**: Attending to all the details of keeping your business running smoothly – attracting clients, blog posts, articles for LinkedIn and other platforms, social media presence, making videos, pod casts, accounting, and on and on. This includes continued learning that hopefully plops you right on the edge of your comfort zone. If you can do this, you'll learn a lot. But if not done properly, you'll feel overwhelmed and hear exhaustion knocking on your door (and hopefully begin to grasp the importance of out-sourcing).

- **Keeping The Home Fires Burning**: Making sure your household runs smoothly. This includes attending to an amazing number of details: food in the frig, changing the cat's litter box, walking the dog, paying bills, doing laundry, house cleaning, changing the sheets on the bed, and on and on. And isn't it amazing how long it seems to take to consistently manage each of these so that everyday life unfolds with a minimal number of glitches? Longing for an efficiency expert (or a maid) may begin to enter the picture.

- **Nurturing Your Relationships**: Continuing to foster your relationships with your own family, your family of origin, and friends. Aside from business demands, this is usually the strongest contender fighting for your energy, focus, and attention. This is where the push/pull dilemma can be felt the strongest. Nothing is more important than family and friends. But ... sometimes it has to be pushed to the side to wait a bit for your attention. When is a good time to do that??? As a loving Mom, partner or friend, is there ever a good time? When is a good time to push your business needs aside for a bit? Is there ever a good time from the entrepreneur's point of view? Hence the stress, worry, and frustration emerge.

What We Forget To Remember

There is another category of demands equally challenging. It's been relegated to something you know you should attend to, but just don't have the time (thanks to the Super Woman gene).

This is the confusing notion of self-care.

I've found most women don't really know what that is. At best, it means making time for our modern day version: exercise, better diet, more conscious attention to what's in our purchases at the grocery store, cooking more, eating out less, watching fewer TV programs, getting enough sleep, maybe even an occasional (or regular) massage!

But there are three additional CORE needs that most female entrepreneurs *absolutely require* and don't remember to weave into their day – every day! Know what they are?

I call these CORE needs the three R's for Female Entrepreneurs: rest, renewal, and reflection.

These are of fundamental importance to business (financial) success and personal happiness.

These three needs live deep in your heart and soul – outside the realm of your thinking mind. When you just keep chewing on your problems and hunting for solutions, you can easily ignore the presence of these deeper needs.

That's when their demand for your attention can expand exponentially. And as weird as it may seem, the heart and soul can create some pretty unpleasant ways to get your attention.

But what does this have to do with being a female entrepreneur? Well, hang in there.

Because I've found it has a lot do with the unique quality of the female entrepreneur's success and failure.

Not responding to the call of these three core needs plops us right into the hands of an everyday dilemma – one that few of us know what to do with, and rarely even recognize as the reason we're feeling so stressed out and overwhelmed. And, if you're not careful, it will negatively impact your business via your financial decisions

The Core Dilemma You Have To Manage Everyday
Do I take care of myself now, or everyone and everything else first,
including my career?

Once you realize that YOU are also a category that must be attended to as well as business and family and friends, the dilemma gets a bit clearer – and more difficult.

As you attempt to manage all of the above details of your professional and personal lives, this dilemma arises as a repeating question – whether you're conscious of it, or not. After all, there are only 24 hours in a day. And that's just not enough time to do it all!

When you add your own needs into the picture, the dilemma gets a bit more complicated. It rearranges itself from just *either* business *or* family/friends to *either* business/family/friends *or* you.

Although the dilemma and the answer will have to change with the circumstances, stress arises from the fact that each time the dilemma arises, you have to make a decision.

In other words, an either/or question demands an answer and a resolution.

As the moments of life unfold, circumstances and situations change. And so does the best way to answer this question.

Becoming conscious of this dilemma (the *either/or* question) and what to do with it when it arises, dramatically reduces your stress, anxiety, doubt, and frustration.

Here are a few common examples of how it creates distress in your business and personal lives:

- Do I do the dishes now or balance my accounts?
- Do I skip my kids' school play tonight or meet for drinks with that potential investor who can help me get out of debt and turn my business around?
- Do I spend my free time this afternoon watching that on-line training on how to get high paying clients, or do I grab these few hours and go grocery shopping which I'm desperate to do?
- Do I keep tweeting and blogging today, or honor my intuition that I really just need a day off, all to myself?
- Do I move away from my computer right now and just sit by the window and watch the rain, or do I stick it out until I get this program to start working again?

These are stressful questions requiring stressful answers. Why?

Whichever option you choose will still leave you wanting,
or needing, to also do the one you didn't choose.

Sometimes life helps out and changes the situation. If your kids' school play is cancelled, part of you is happy because now you won't miss the joy of seeing it. And you're free to meet with the potential Mr. Money Bags without guilt.

But of course, that rarely happens, right?

So you're left with an additional layer of stress that comes from making decisions you don't want to make in the first place.

Is There A Way Out?

Is there a better way to manage these dilemmas? Well, you still have to make a decision. That's life. BUT ... there is a way to navigate this sticky situation without feeling guilt, stress, or frustration about the option you DIDN'T choose.

In other words, you can learn how to feel good even though you're feeling bad about your choice!
And that is truly essential for staying on top of an entrepreneurial life.

This ability becomes available when you learn how to shift your attention. You want to move your attention away from the dilemma and its accompanying stress. Instead, you want to place it on fulfilling your three core needs: rest, renewal, and reflection.

Move them right up to the top of the priorities list. And with just a few little tricks, you can leave that guilt, stress, and frustration behind.

First: Play The *'As If'* Game

Remembering you have core needs rests in a little trick you may have to practice. It's easy once you get the knack for the *'As If'* game. The trick is simple:

- *Imagine as if* you really KNOW that the 'best' answer cannot arise out of stress, anxiety, or frustration – especially choices relating to your bottom line.
- *Imagine as if* you KNOW your best answer in the moment is alive and well and available by turning

your attention to resting, renewing, and reflecting.

You see, your brain does everything it can to make what you think is true actually FEEL true. When this happens, you can comfortably make the choice that feels right to you without guilt or frustration.

Thoughts that leave you in conflict about which choice is the better one breed anxiety and doubt. You can change conflicting thoughts into positive ones that let you feel better about having to choose one option over the other. Using the *As If* game as I noted above is a great way to do this.

> *And the positive thought we're talking about is this:*
> *the answer to your dilemma will be there for you when you fulfill*
> *your three core needs.*

What can undermine this game is buying into the belief that you're new positive thought isn't true. You'll hear something like: *'Getting some rest, renewing, and reflecting is not going to change anything!'*

Your mind will scan all the evidence it can find to support the negative view: continually rising debt, number of clients decreasing, strategy for generating social media presence not working, etc.

> *BUT ... if you understand the 'As If' game provides the groundwork for your brain to make the positive thought <u>feel truer</u> than the negative thought, you've won the challenge.*

Not to be too repetitive, but here's the positive thought once again: the answer to your dilemma will be there for you when you fulfill your three core needs.

Second: Take Four Precise Steps
Follow these steps and you'll find yourself ready to access your core needs.

♥ **Acknowledge You Can't Wish Away Your Stress**

There is no point in kidding yourself. Feeling overwhelmed is the most common experience of all entrepreneurs. So just take a breath and acknowledge you *are* feeling stressed.

Prove it to yourself by noticing the tension in your body, whether or not you're holding your breath, if you're feeling anxious, angry, frustrated, sad, hopeless, or helpless. Face up to the fact that this is where you're at right now. You can't manage what you won't allow yourself to recognize.

This is often the hardest step to take. The drive that made you want to become a female entrepreneur in the first place will not want to admit to what it sees as potential weakness or failure.

It's your challenge to remember weakness is only the precursor to strength.

For example, the muscle fibers in your body work together. They are not antagonistic. They actually complement each other. They efficiently keep your body both standing and moving via contraction and relaxation. Weakness and strength work together as well. They're a powerful duo dedicated to stoking the fires of motivation and commitment so they burn strong and long.

♥ Grant Yourself Permission To Indulge In The Three R's

Do you find yourself too often waiting for others to give you permission to breathe, to do what you know you need to do? Do you want others to grant you their approval or agreement, or to acquiesce to your need as being more important than theirs?

The Super Woman gene has a built-in resistance to recognizing the only person's permission you actually need to rest, renew, and reflect is your own.

No matter how scary it may seem to give yourself this time, keep playing the 'As If' game. KNOW the gifts (I'll list them for you in a minute) you'll receive from taking the time to rest, renew, and reflect far exceed anything else you could do for others or for yourself (and for your bottom line).

♥ Inform Others Of Your Decision

Let everyone who'll be affected by your time out know that you are going to take a short break – away from them or the situation. You don't need to explain it. You just need to declare it as so.

Use the tools that respond to email telling folks you're away from your desk for a while. And remember, it's not the end of your business (or your world) if you don't respond to your emails and texts immediately! Set your own limit for how long it's ok to wait before responding. I find the majority of clients will adjust.

Be respectful of others and their dependence on you. But remain firm in your commitment to making time for honoring and accessing your own core needs. The fulfillment of these needs holds the resolution to that dilemma this entire article is addressing.

♥ Know These Actions ARE Self-Care

Imagine as if these actions will take care of your stress. Engaging in rest and renewal, and creating time for reflection and contemplation don't lead to self-care. They ARE self-care in action.

You don't have to do anything else. Your body and mind are each equipped to naturally restore balance physically, mentally, and emotionally (the goal of self-care). You don't have to do it for your mind and body. They know how to activate the effects of self-care on their own. All you need to do is rest, renew (relax), and reflect.

When you're stressed out, angry, anxious, or frustrated, the frontal lobe of your brain is not in the lead. That's the part of your brain that handles all executive functioning and critical thinking.

Instead, the 'fight or flight' dictate behind stress is being generated by your amygdala, or your primitive brain at the back of your skull. You need your frontal lobe to kick back in and take over. Taking the time to fill your core needs allows that to happen naturally.

Your heart and soul/spirit are also equipped with an innate drive to be happy and carefree. Again, you don't have to do it for them. You just have to give your heart and soul/spirit the time and space to do what they know how to do. Then you just show up and enjoy.

Core Needs Balance Your Drive To Care For The Other & To Care For Yourself
As women, we are blessed with a natural desire to infuse our lives with love, compassion, and caring. That's a beautiful thing. But does that increase our financial bottom line – the core concern for all entrepreneurs?

You've probably been enticed by a very common notion that actualizing love, compassion and caring requires you to 'be' and to 'do' things in a certain way.

Insisting your actions *always* reflect love, compassion and caring for others can produce a lot of confusion and frustration. Juggling the fulfillment of your personal needs and the needs of everything else in your life just isn't that simple.

This is an inner tug-of-war that is particularly strong in our feminine hearts. Not only are we *conditioned* to be caretakers, it is the natural bent of the female psyche to rise above fight or flight and to *befriend*. But when you do that too much, your gross income may go into cardiac arrest!

This befriending aspect tips the 'me or you' scales to an imbalanced position. You may be left wondering what to do with *your* desires at the end of the day when there is no more time or energy left.

Women have come a long way at moving differently in the outer world. But most of us still feel confusion or nagging doubt in the inner world that something is not yet fully right.

Melody's Story
Melody is a 35-year-old entrepreneur with a 3-year-old professional

editing business. She is also a self-professed supermom with a traveling husband, and a couple of kids to take care of, as well as a cat named Gorgeous George and a dog named Mr. Tex.

She was convinced that having her own business would be the icing on the cake. She longed for the freedom she believed came with being her own boss. Melody was certain it was the key to her fulfillment and happiness. Yet when she came to see me, anxiety was her constant companion and her stress level was off the charts.

One day, desperate for relief, Melody flew into my office, gripping her Starbuck's coffee cup so tightly I thought she was going to crumble it and slosh coffee everywhere.

She literally threw herself onto my couch and began to cry. *"I try my best, but I just can't keep things under control. I can't keep my partner happy, the kids focused on school, the house clean, enough money in my business account, and stay sane. Tell me what I'm doing wrong."*

She grabbed the Kleenex box, wiped her nose, and continued: *"I can't deal with all the choices I have to make every day. There has to be a better way! My life is driving me crazy!"*

I knew Melody wanted to be happy. For that to happen she needed to find some wisdom about what was going on. She had to find a practical way to better manage her responsibilities.

She told me she wanted to stay calm and make decisions without going in circles, worrying if her choices were right or wrong. Here's a few of the decisions she was facing on a pretty regular basis:

> • pick up the kids' clothes or leave them lying around for a day
> • cook good organic food for dinner or eat out at a fast-food restaurant
> • finish the art project out in the garage or go to the networking event
> • have coffee with her friends or hang out at home by herself

- go over her finances or go to the movies

Melody goes in circles because she wants to feel good and pick the right choice to get her there. But not knowing how to manage these dilemmas (either/or decisions) makes feeling good impossible.

These dilemmas can leave you feeling paralyzed, corner you into arguments, catch you in a power trip, amplify your desire to control things, debilitate your health, rob you of the courage you need to stand up for yourself, create exhaustion, turn you into a workaholic or codependent, hook you into other addictive behaviors, and block you from doing what actually needs to be done to keep your business thriving.

All of this can and usually does happen. But only because you may remain unaware or unable to access your core needs for rest, renewal, and reflection.

When Melody learned how to access these deeper needs, things began to change. She discovered she could stop fretting over whether her solutions were right or wrong when she faced an either/or decision.

That's because she now had new resources at her fingertips. As promised, let's take a look at the gifts Melody received by accessing her three core needs on a consistent basis.

The Gifts of Rest, Renewal, and Reflection
Your capacity for rest, renewal and reflection must be activated in order for you to receive the following cornucopia of gifts. This activation simply requires your presence. YOU are the key. Focusing your attention is what triggers the release of these presents.

Many powerful and supportive gifts rest within you and are always available to assist in the decision making essential to both professional and financial success as well as personal happiness.

Your only job is to invite them forth via rest, renewal, and reflection.

The following are twelve of these highly prized gifts essential to the continuity of motivation, commitment, and tenacity essential to your professional accomplishments:

1. **Wisdom** - the intelligent application of your current life learnings. Wisdom draws out a deeper knowing and understanding that triggers a new level of creativity into action. Wisdom offers encouragement and a sense of emotional safety. Wisdom guides you to learn from your personal experience. This wisdom remains out of reach when your body is in the grips of stress and worry.
2. **Calm** – a sense of relative freedom from anxiety and skeletal muscle tension. Renewal stimulates the parasympathetic nervous system and a return to greater physical calmness and emotional stability via the relaxation response. Stress stimulates the sympathetic nervous system and the fight or flight response that keeps your decision making rooted in worry and fear.
3. **Trust** – the balancing factor to doubt. Trust generates a confidence in the reliability and availability of your own inner guidance, as well as the positive value of doubt. This accelerates your willingness to schedule time for rest, renewal, and reflection into your daily routine. Without trust, the three R's can become just a distant thought.
4. **Faith** – the result of discovering how trust and doubt work together to keep you present, mindful, and willing to access your inner sense of knowing that there is a best decision for you in each new situation. Faith opens the door to new angles of vision and freedom to contemplate seemingly impossible possibilities. Without it, giving up can enter the scene.
5. **Clarity** – seeing with sharpness, lucidity, and coherence. The ability to allow the issue in question to be not only a problem or challenge but also part of the larger whole working for you. For example, let's say you have a favorite tapestry hanging in your office. Stress results when you focus on the tiny flaw you just noticed in the lower left

corner. You worry about how to fix it. Clarity shifts your focus to the presence of the whole tapestry, or the bigger picture. Focusing on the whole that holds the flaw within it opens the door to new perspectives and options previously unseen. Without clarity, confusion reigns.

6. **Joy** –a happy and delightful state of mind that redirects the heart to cheerfulness and a warm delight. This changes your physiology and brain chemistry allowing you greater access to your frontal lobe and the critical thinking so essential to effective decision-making. Without an occasional dose of joy, business becomes an unwelcome burden.

7. **Guidance** – directions from a higher aspect of yourself. Until you connect with this inner guidance, it remains just a lovely notion. But once you've touched its' presence within yourself, you can more easily let go of stressing out. In this way you create space for the best way to handle the situation to arise.

8. **Gratitude** – a feeling of thankfulness for the reality of your own inner guidance, which can only emerge when you are rested, relaxing, and reflecting. Again, gratitude impacts your chemistry and physiology moving you away from stress and toward the awesome fact that you are alive.

9. **Strength** – the granting of fortitude. Strength is the determination to resist being moved or at worse, shattered, by an external circumstance or internal negativity. Strength is called forth most easily by acknowledging the presence of weakness.

10. **Courage** – a unique quality of mind or spirit that allows you to stand up to difficulties, pain, and experiences of loss without allowing fear to take the lead. Courage is called forth most easily by acknowledging the presence of fear and trembling deep within.

11. **Understanding** – the power to comprehend, mentally grasp, interpret or explain the current circumstance from a different and usually larger perspective. This allows more room for creative action to arise. Understanding sheds lights on dark situations and offers new avenues of resolution that can't be found in the dark.

12. **Insight** – to catch, in a flash, a glimpse of the inner nature of

a situation, what it's all about, and what you are to learn from its presence. Insight often combines all of the above gifts in a swift flash of understanding, clarity, and gratitude that leave strength, courage, trust, faith, and wisdom reverberating in its wake.

The Most Important Bottom Line Is Fulfilling Your Core Needs

Too many bad decisions, financial and otherwise, arise out of the stress and frustration that accompany dilemmas. The way around this is consistently dedicating time to the three R's.

This is so easy that it's actually difficult. We're just not used to taking care of our core needs because all they actually require is our presence – not thinking *about* them, but being *with* them. That gives them all the room they need to do their thing.

So here's the scoop:

Just sit down. Stop doing. Stop being an entrepreneur. Stop thinking about problems and their solutions. Stop worrying about money and your branding.

Switch the focus of your attention to reflecting on what's going on in the exact moment you're in. Is what's happening in your awareness the sound of the wind, the traffic, the growling in your stomach, the feel of the surface you're sitting on?

Whatever it is, approach it with the same exploratory view as your tongue does when it rolls over the space where your tooth used to be. It's trying to get a feel for the space, the size of it, what's there and what's not.

Your tongue doesn't need to draw any conclusions. It's just getting a feel for what is new and different. Likewise, you don't need to draw any conclusions either. Just let your mind contemplate or reflect on what's in front of it. It's still thinking but it's not problem/solution focused. It's like meandering down a country lane or a city street when you're not in a hurry. There's nothing to do and nowhere to be.

Don't make it difficult. It isn't. You're just not used to allowing another aspect of you some time to discover and explore itself. Even though it doesn't seem logical, this is the process that grants you the best way to manage the decision making around those either/or questions.

And this is the single most powerful way to stay calm whether your financial success is going through a challenging downtime or a joyous upswing.

Some people meditate, pray, read poetry or fill up with other words that inspire. Perhaps you're a lover of mindfulness. That will do too. There's just nothing easier (and harder) than simply being here and being now.

Whatever you do, stay with the notion that there's really nothing for you to do here. Just give your three core needs some time and space. They'll grant you so much in return you'll start making them an everyday priority you wouldn't miss for the world.

About the Author

Ragini Elizabeth Michaels has been a certified trainer of NLP (Neuro-Linguistic Programming) and Waking Hypnosis since 1989. During 4 decades of successful private practice, Ragini was also certified as a Life and Personal Wellness Coach and Spiritual Life Coach.

Ragini is the author of 4 books: *Facticity – a door to mental health & beyond,* an introduction to the reality and difficulties of 'either/or' dilemmas. Next came *Lions In Wait – a road to personal courage,* a trance storybook created specifically to share with therapists and hypnotherapists. Next came *Unflappable – 6 Steps To Staying Happy, Centered and Peaceful No Matter What,* precise step-by-step guidance for how to defuse the stress and frustration created by *either/or* dilemmas. And finally *The Wildly Quiet Presence of God,* a compilation of 40 heartfelt musings paired with beautiful images to touch the heart and soul.

From 1988 to 2000, Ragini taught throughout Europe and India as well as running a private vocational school in Seattle, Washington. She offered certification training in NLP, Ericksonian Hypnosis, and her original contribution to NLP called Paradox Management.

She continued her passion for discovering how to better handle the abundance of dilemmas and double binds intrinsic to everyday life. From 2000 to 2010 she headed the Paradox Management Wisdom School offering training and guidance in what she has coined the *Dirty Dozen Dilemmas Of Everyday Life*.

To get a copy of her free *The Three R's Workbook: Check List & Action Guide* based on her contribution in this book, go to www.raginimichaels.com/3-R-Workbook.

Coaching Website: www.BottomLineCoaching.net
Training Websites: www.ToHelpYouHelpOthers.com &
www.RaginiMichaels.com
Email: Ragini@BottomLineCoaching.net
Phone: 001 425 462 4369

Women Entrepreneurs Have a Competitive Edge
By Don L. Morgan, PhD

Survivability is not the norm when it comes to new businesses. According to *The Entrepreneur's Toolkit,* seven out of ten new businesses fail within the first few years. Only 20 percent make it beyond five years. The upshot is that these dire statistics can be overcome with a few relatively simple strategies that focus on developing vital allies and listening to reduce their blind spots. For female entrepreneurs, the news is even better because they have an advantage in cultivating these strategies and beating the odds.

Initially, I didn't understand why I was asked to write a chapter for this book. I thought that a female coach would be better suited. After speaking with other coaches, I realized why I was offered this opportunity. Most of the life coaches I know are women and the majority of my coaching clients at Positivity Academy are female. I must say, I have found women to be more receptive to the idea of working with a coach and the most enterprising women I have worked with want to hear all points of view, male and female.

Women as Leaders
Through my work with the Positivity Academy, I have gained a look at the future, and it is obvious to me that women are emerging as the vital business leaders of tomorrow. The future is now. In March of 2013, a *Los Angeles Times* article stated that "Women leaders are more likely than men to consider competing interests and take a cooperative approach when making decisions." They are also "more inquisitive than men and tend to see more than one solution to a problem."

I have certainly found this to be the case in my work at Positivity Academy. The leadership attributes that I teach are more common among women. In his book, *The Landmarks of Tomorrow,* Peter Drucker emphasizes the virtues of inquisitiveness — of asking questions — when it comes to working effectively with others and observed that women are "usually better" at working with others than are men. People must inform their colleagues about what they are doing, why and how. In turn, they need to ask these things of their associates. Statistically speaking, women are better corporate leaders than men.

"Knowledge workers" — a term coined by Drucker — are workers whose main capital is knowledge, such as scientists, engineers, doctors, pharmacists, accountants, lawyers, teachers, professors, administrators, and any worker whose job requires one to "think for a living."

Human Interaction Management has identified 5 principles of knowledge work:
1. Build effective teams.
2. Communicate in a structured way.
3. Create, share and maintain knowledge.
4. Align your time with strategic goals.
5. Negotiate next steps as you work.

Drucker suggests that "the most valuable asset of a 21st-century institution, whether business or non-business, will be its knowledge workers and their productivity." Women tend to be more nurturing than men and are often more effective than are their male counterparts. By nature, many women are very well suited to be successful entrepreneurs and to improve the odds of success for new businesses.

The Johari Window
The Johari Window emphasizes some of the most important qualities of humanity. In 1965 at the University of California Los Angeles, psychologists, Harry Ingham and Joseph Luft crafted the Johari Window to explain behavior and awareness. This psychological model is also helpful for assessing and improving a group's relationship with other groups. One of the major factors exposed is that of the blind spot.

	Known by Self	Unknown by Self
Known by Others	**ARENA** (Public, Open)	**BLIND SPOT**
Unknown by Others	**FAÇADE** (Avoided, Hidden)	**UNKNOWN**

Reduce Blind Spots with Conceptual Diversity

Do you know what you bring to the table? Do you know what others are capable of contributing? Blind spots are invisible. No matter how intelligent you are, you can't see what you can't see. And what you can't see does not exist in your world. Reducing one's blind spot is vital for building for survivability and for generating profitability. Competitive people, and especially highly task-oriented women fall into habitual ways of seeing the world. This focus is what makes them so special. To be even more effective as leaders, they will listen to the unique ideas and perspectives of their vital allies.

As an entrepreneur, it is critical to reduce the size of your blind spot by identifying and cultivating vital connections—people with different mindsets. Awareness of several ways of seeing is essential for business success. Four identifiable perspectives that can reduce an entrepreneur's blind spot are:

1. A mindset focused on outcomes and results (D-Dominance).
2. A mindset striving for positive interactions with others (i-Influence).
3. A mindset concerned with the workplace environment (S-Steadiness).
4. A mindset based on adherence to established standards (C-Compliance).

There are many assessment systems that grew out of Jungian theory. Psychologists who study personality traits have concluded that there are few, if any, people-types with well-defined boundaries into which folks can be unambiguously placed. People differ, but these differences are of degree and not of kind. We all have options to behave as Introverts or Extroverts, as optimists or pessimists. There is no firm line between introversion and extraversion. We all have access to a wide array of traits, and yet we tend to use some more than others.

DiSC trait profiling was suggested by William Moulton Marston in his 1928 book, *Emotions of Normal People*. Industrial psychologist Walter Clarke used Marston's DiSC model to develop the Activity Vector Analysis for businesses to select qualified employees. It was expanded by John Geier in 1958 in his Performax Learning Network Profiles. Each behavioral style carries a habitual perspective and reactive feedback to issues and plans.

In 1972, John Geier published the original Personal Profile (DiSC) System. DiSC (lower case i) is the original Performax assessment instrument developed by John Geier. DiSC assessment has been used by more than 50 million people. It is especially helpful for learning about one's self and for working with other people. Geier's Performax scale has three sets of profiles for each person. The first profile is the usual pattern of behavior in normal situations. Geier's second profile set identifies traits that emerge under pressure. A third profile is a composite or hybrid combining the two other assessments.

Life Coaches and Football Coaches Employ All Four Behavioral Styles
The value of a professional life coach is based on the ability to activate the most effective thinking style for dealing with your potential blind spots. When it comes to interactive styles, life coaching is not that different from football coaching. A football coach activates and works at behaviors to contribute to the success of the team.

Consider the following coaching functions:

D-Style: A football coach selects people for their natural abilities to play each of the positions. Selecting the best plays to run and uniforms to order for next season. As an entrepreneur, you will benefit from interaction with someone who focuses on the big picture — who is concerned about the bottom line and who makes good decisions under pressure. D-type tendencies include:

- Direct, say what they think.
- Ask, "What's the bottom line?"
- Focus on the big picture.
- Impatience, make decisions quickly.
- Make good decisions when under pressure.
- Developing organizational structure and control.

i-Style: Spontaneous generation of enthusiasm is vital before games and at halftime. **i**-type behavior generates positivity, team communication, action, and inspiration. Entrepreneurs benefit by being talkative — even animated at times. It is essential for entrepreneurs to inspire their stakeholders, just as football coaches inspire their players. I-type descriptors include:

- Open and friendly, people person.
- Talkative, animated, excitable and comfortable with physical touch.
- Short attention span and less concerned with details.
- Spontaneous and enthusiastic.
- May appear disorganized and repeats questions.
- Positive communicators, active, and inspirational.

S-Style: Football coaches can be possessive of physical space by authorizing or rejecting use of the stadium. They set behavioral standards for their locker room. Their understanding and empathy contribute to team loyalty. Morgan's college football coach covered his tuition, found a part-time job for him during the school year, and engineered a great summer job with Union Pacific Railroad. Boise head coach Lyle Smith also demonstrated concern and support for injured players and for those with personal problems. Just as football coaches build loyalty, entrepreneurs benefit by S-

Style behaviors:

- Easy-going, calm, not easily excited.
- Good listener — pays attention.
- Asks questions about specifics.
- Thoughtful, likes to think about things.
- Possessive of physical space.
- Withholds strong opinions.
- Steady and slow to change.
- Caring and showing understanding and empathy.

C-Style: Football coaches focus on detail. People guessed that Vince Lombardi, famous coach of the Green Bay Packers, was a High-D. But his DiSC results showed that he scored higher on both Compliance and Influence styles. Successful coaches study specifications and issues. They criticize player performance and make decisions based on fact, not opinion. Football coaches insist on following the rules of the game and demand class attendance. They adhere to regulations and spot unanticipated consequences. They pay attention to field conditions, air temperature, and wind conditions. They consider the surroundings and environment, analyze problems, and handle issues thoroughly. An entrepreneur needs C-style thinking:

- Quiet, focused on detail.
- Cautious, asks many questions.
- Reserved, appears a bit shy.
- Carefully studies specifications and issues.
- Offers criticism and makes decisions based on fact, not opinion.
- Follows regulations and spots unanticipated consequences.
- Aware of surroundings, analyze problems, and handle issues thoroughly.

Identifying and Recruiting Vital Allies

To reduce the magnitude of your blind spot, seek out and interact with your vital contacts. This can include an accountant, a lawyer, a professional life coach, a casual acquaintance, a relative, or just about anyone fitting each of the DiSC styles.

Where do you find people to serve as your vital contacts? Family and friends can be helpful. Surprisingly, you can find even more help from your "Weak Ties" — casual acquaintances and friends of friends. Connecting with weak-tie acquaintances is probably more important because it gives you access to new social networks. Often, weak-tie acquaintances are more influential than are your close-tie friends.

As an entrepreneur, you operate from a future-oriented mindset. Family and friends typically operate from a historical mindset. It is important to be aware of these limitations. People who care about you want to keep you from making mistakes. They look for problems, weaknesses, and threats. When parting, you can hear them say, "Be safe, drive carefully." "Don't do anything that I wouldn't do!"

Never ask for advice about what to do or not do. Ask for options to consider or about their feelings. If you ask what you should do and then you do something else, they will feel that you don't respect their ideas. It is better to ask for several ideas to consider.

Discourage "Should-ing" and "Ought-ing." You are not asking what to do. You need to know what they like and what they don't like. In working with your vital contacts, seek feedback on likes and dislikes.

Explain that mistakes are to be seen as teachers to learn from. Rephrase problems into challenges. To alter the context, look at challenges as opportunities. Ask "How might we _____?

"*Might*" is a strength-based term for possibilities. (*Might* = Power, strength, valor, force, permission, can, may, influence, and force.)

The best way to reach out beyond your family and friends is to ask:
- "Who do you know that can _____?"
- "Who do you know that knows a lot about _____?"
- "Who do you know that can help me think through some business decisions?"

Professional Life Coaches are Client-Centered

Just like football coaches, professional life coaches demonstrate interactive styles appropriate to shrink client blind spots and to act as catalysts for client flourishing. By asking strategic open questions, life coaches learn when and where to take on the style congruent with the issues of their clients. Typical questions and comments to entrepreneurial clients include:

- How are your products different from or better than that of your competition?
- How do you price your products?
- Who are your potential customers?
- How are you going to market your products?
- Tell me about product production and delivery.
- How do you retain your customers?
- What are the 5 things you must do to be successful?

For many entrepreneurs, one of the most valuable functions of a life coach is to provide accountability. There is research that found that people who share their *New Year's Resolutions* with their priests or rabbis tend to follow through with their resolutions to a much greater extent than do those who do not share their resolutions with such professionals.

Not all professional life coaches have the training or experience to assist in all situations. A client described a health-related issue and asked her coach what should she do. The response, "Second opinions are only valuable from experts in the field. After a few days and talking to several others, you will make the best decision possible."

Dr. Morgan's Positivity Academy provides training and materials for several life coaching specialties. Membership in the International Association of Professional Life Coaches provides a network of referral options. Additionally, you can expect coaches to recommend specialists from other professions. Professional Life Coaches adhere to a code of ethics that requires confidentiality.

Life Coaching and Athletic Coaching are Different

Athletic coaches rely on telling and yelling. Life coaches rely on asking and listening. The following diagram presents a simplified picture of SMART questions used in PositivityAcademy.com coach training.

S M A R T Business Questions
Specific: What is the Big Dream goal that you plan to achieve?
Metrics: What is the Cost estimate? Time required? Completion date? Proof of success?
Alignment: How does this goal fit with your values? What is your "Why"?
Resources: What resources are available? What resources are needed?
Threats: What are the roadblocks, detours, and hurdles that threaten goal achievement?

A question asked in the right way often points to its own answer. Asking questions is the ABC of coaching. If you don't ask the right questions, you don't get the right answers.

Ms. Boss

As an entrepreneur, you are the CEO, the big boss of your business. Research has shown that "companies with at least one female director were 20 percent less likely to file bankruptcy." Also, those with "higher representations of females on their boards had better financial performance."

Leadership includes taking uncomfortable roles. Your vital role as a leader will emerge from attentive listening. When you sense that the other person is exhausted or losing sight of the goal, you can adopt an i-style and become a cheerleader of sorts. To provide support for someone who is discouraged, go into an S-Style mode. This includes active listening and giving feedback to show understanding of the plight of the other party.

C-Style behaviors also have a place in an entrepreneur's tool box. Here you can ask questions: "Do you foresee any problems? Are there any regulations that bear on the situation? What kind of problems have other people encountered? What is a possible downside or unanticipated consequence of such an action?" Many times, all that is needed is a clear decision or specific direction. This is where D-Style is the most effective leadership behavior, and is an appropriate mindset for a business owner.

In his book, *Pursuing the Good Life,* Dr. Chris Peterson, primary author of VIA Character Strengths Assessment observed:

> It is impossible to draw a firm line along the continuum, despite heroic attempts in psychiatric diagnosis, which assume that there are types of people: those with the disorder and those without. There are no character types except in theory, just people who have more versus less of a given strength. No matter what character strengths we considered, the results were unanimous in supporting a dimensional rather than a categorical view of character strengths. The differences are of degree and not of kind. All of us can move from the more sinful end of things to the more-saintly end, no matter where we start, because there are no barriers of kind over which we must leap.

You have the opportunity to choose which traits to activate based on your appraisal of the situation. In other words, the DiSC measures are not traits but are habit related tendencies. In a one-to-one interaction, you have the option of selecting which traits to utilize. You can change your focus. You have the capability to shift gears. In the process of being an essential contact for another, the most valuable trait clusters to activate or use or react from can be uncomfortable.

Vital Leadership

In a large corporation, a major factor in one's success is to know her unique strengths and to work on developing her talents to promote company goals. For entrepreneurs, a major factor for success is acknowledgment of one's personality traits and blind spots, and to work at ways to fill the perceptual gaps in planning and decision-making. In our team-building seminars, one of our most important outcomes is a sense of conceptual diversity — instilling greater appreciation for other people's contributions.

Confidential Sounding Board

By telling your coach about an idea or planned course of action, either you will become even more committed to an action or you will go back to the drawing board. This function of a professional coach is most valuable for decision-maker. Going public prematurely with an idea that can negatively affect stakeholders' opinion of a leader.

One of our coaching tools is *Root Cause Analysis*, commonly called the *5 Whys*. By repeating the question, "And what will that get you?" Coaches provide clients with both a microscope and the telescope to see their malleable futures. As the architect of your future, your professional life coach can provide the right questions for you to make better choices.

Questions are the Answer

One of the most important reasons for an entrepreneur to work with a professional coach is to learn how the coach uses questions to guide thinking. Even more important, when a concept is developed or refined by you answering a coach's questions, you have ownership of the idea. Coaches are not for selling action plans. They are not after your "buy-in." It is important for you to own your mission, and it is important to learn to build loyalty and commitment in your people by asking the right questions and listening to their views.

Summary

> While only 20 percent of new businesses make it beyond five years, female entrepreneurs have a competitive edge in cultivating the necessary strategies to beat the odds.

> All entrepreneurs have blind spots. Because entrepreneurs are the decision-makers of their respective businesses, there is value in the feedback from others with their unique views.

> Other mindsets can reduce an entrepreneur's blind spot and

are vital for business success.

- A mindset focused on outcomes and results (D-Dominance).
- A mindset striving for positive interactions with others (i-Influence).
- A mindset concerned with the work environment (S-Steadiness).
- A mindset based on adherence to established standards (C-Compliance).

➢ DiSC is a behavior assessment tool based on William Moulton Marston's 1928 book called *The Emotions of Normal People*. He theorized that people express their emotions using 4 possible behavior styles: Dominance (D), Inducement (I), Submission (S), and Compliance (C). Women are more nurturing by nature and are more likely to exhibit inspirational, supportive, and compliance perspectives.

➢ There is a never-ending contest between past and future mindsets. Advice and suggestions from family members and from friends tend to take on a "past" mindset. Consultations with professionals tend to take a future oriented mindset. Through strategic questioning, a Professional Life Coach can identify and adopt approaches congruent with any missing mindset perspectives.

➢ Asking the right questions is an essential skill for an entrepreneur's business success. You can learn this skill by working with a professional life coach.

About the Author

Don L. Morgan, PhD, Positive Psychology Practitioner, holds certificates in a number of areas, including Leader Effectiveness Training, Executive Coach, Master Life Coach, Master Business Coach, Motivational Interviewing, and Law of Attraction Practitioner. Morgan was certified by John Geier as a Performax Phase III Consultant (highest level) on August 21, 1981. He has participated in all five World Congress of Positive Psychology conferences held every two years.

Don started his professional career as an athletic coach and social studies teacher in Melba, Idaho. After a year working as a marketing consultant for a Denver company and 6 years as a secondary teacher and coach, he moved into the principal's office in Amana (Iowa) High School. Two years later he accepted work as a consultant for the University of Iowa. Upon completion of his PhD Morgan joined the Research Learning Center at Clarion State College as Assistant Director for Field Services.

During his 31-year tenure at Clarion University, Professor Morgan served in a variety positions including teaching professional practicum, supervising student teachers, operating an experimental school for elementary and high school students, teaching management classes, counseling, and as Director of Cooperative Education and Internships.

Morgan's work with the Positivity Academy involves coaching and training Positivity Coaches and Organizational Consultants. He thrives on seeing his clients achieve their goals.

> For every problem under the sun,
>
> There is a fix or there is none.
>
> If there be a fix, seek til you find it.
>
> If there is none, never mind it.

Instagram: @positivityacademy
drdomo@comcast.net
PositivityAcademy.com

Behind Every Good Woman...
By Carolyn R Owens

The number of female entrepreneurs has been growing rapidly over the past few years. Freedom is often one of the main reasons why women choose entrepreneurship. They no longer have to worry about getting the next promotion or someone dictating their hours to them. It also offers the opportunity to work in an area they are truly passionate about and able to fully use their talents.

Stepping into the world of entrepreneurship can be a little frightening. With it comes its own set of challenges, some of which are unique to women. I am sure you have at least heard one the success stories of Yang Lan, Oprah Winfrey, Sara Blakely, or J.K. Rowling. You have heard all about their net worth, but what you don't hear is the journey it took to get where they are. Not just the surface stories, but also the late-night tears, feelings of loneliness, the rejection and hurt, the desire to quit, and the resolve to keep going.

As entrepreneurs, we will all have our own story to tell. But the good thing is, now we don't have to go it alone. Coaching is a way to help you tap fully into your creativity and bring your ideas to the surface. It's a way to help you create the business and life of your dreams. It's all about success on YOUR own terms.

Even with the increase in popularity, many women have not heard of coaching, let alone know the benefits of how it can help you. Although coaching and mentoring are quite different, most women have never even had a mentor in the workplace or as a business owner. To clarify, the difference is a mentor has been there and done that. A mentor has had similar but more extensive experience, and guides the mentee through "the ropes." They have connections and are well respected in their industry. Mentors willingly share their experience and knowledge.

As with the mentoring relationship, the client-coach relationship is a partnership based on confidentiality and trust. With coaching, there is not a need for a shared experience or similar knowledge base. A coach supports you to see past what you can see. They teach, guide and are committed to helping you achieve your goals.

Now that you have an idea of what coaching is, at least from my viewpoint, I would like to share with you a little of my journey. I'll share some of the things I've learned along the way. From my experiences and working with clients, you can learn how coaching can help women entrepreneurs be successful on their own terms.

I first heard of coaching just before I retired from military service. I had been coaching and mentoring for years but never knew there was a coaching profession. Although I had people who looked out for me, I never really had a coach or a mentor. I had to figure it out mostly on my own. I did, however, become a mentor and coach for many whom I served with and met along the way.

Coaching and mentoring, along with training, was the part of my career I truly enjoyed. When I learned it was a viable career path, I knew it was what I wanted to do in my next phase of my life. I planned it all out, outlining the steps I needed to take. At the time I didn't know, documenting my transition would turn out to be an Amazon #1 bestseller, *"Your Itty Bitty Heading Home Book: 15 Simple Steps To A Successful Military Transition."*

You might call me naive, but I also didn't know being a coach, working for myself, was running a business. After serving in the military for over 24 years, I would have to learn a whole new world, a whole new culture. What the heck did I know about running a business?

I quickly learned, there were assumptions made if I led with being a female business owner versus being a veteran. Just like when I served in the military, women are judged a certain way. It was another complex environment for me to navigate my way through. How many times did I want to quit? Too many to mention. Having a clear vision, knowing exactly what I wanted helped to fuel my passion to create a life I truly desired. For me, it is a life that is constantly evolving. I learned that's what suites me best.

Having received and delivered some of the best leadership training while in the military, I incorporated those skills into my coaching practice. As my business developed, I met other female entrepreneurs and career professionals who struggled with particular challenges. I encouraged them to consider working with me as their coach. Once they did, they began to focus their time and energy on what they truly wanted their business and life to look like. Some changed career paths. Some started businesses. What they chose to do didn't matter. They were ready to live life out loud.

Here are a few of the common challenges I observed. This will enable you to recognize them if they show up with your business.

> **Not thinking strategically.** Women entrepreneurs often operate from a place of intuition and trust. I have seen too many women who will agree to things before getting all the details. They end up discovering "the project" is not in alignment with their plans. However, they feel obligated to finish "the project" which results in taking time and resources away from building their business.
>
> Women entrepreneurs often end up being taken advantage of, especially when first getting started. A person may want to do business with you but will tell you that because you are just getting started or because you are not making a certain amount of income, you should do all the work for free. They may even offer to barter services with you. If you were to really take a look at what is being offered, it is not a fair deal.
>
> There are times when it will make sense to do things for free, but you have to know how this fits in with your business plan. You must have a clearly defined vision. You must know exactly where you are now, where you want to go, and create a plan to get there. Don't just keep it all in your

head. Write it down and review the plan regularly. A coach can assist you in developing your vision and plan of action. They can also hold you accountable.

Overwhelm and frustration. When I first started my business, entrepreneur and radio show host, Patsy Anderson, said to me "Most women walk away just before they hit success. What they don't realize is that they are right on the edge. Just one more step and they would have hit success but they quit too soon." I also heard by the three-year mark, most small businesses fail. Motivating words to hear, right?

It is the overwhelm and frustration that consumes someone and leads them to give up. A large part of this comes from not setting priorities. Actually, it's not knowing what your priorities are in the first place. Setting priorities can be hard to figure out because you just don't know where to start. You end up feeling so far behind, you feel as if you will never catch up.

Coaching can help you get organized. You can work with a coach to create your vision and then set yearly, monthly, weekly and daily goals for your business. You will create a roadmap that serves as your guide along the entrepreneurial journey.

Self-sabotaging behaviours. We are a product of our experiences. These experiences create our belief system. There are behaviours we are taught as young girls that become ingrained in us impacting our communication and leadership styles. They impact our thinking, speaking, and engagement as a business owner. These can be unconscious behaviours our customers, clients, and business associates are watching and passing judgment about our abilities. A great example is when you shake someone's hand. Do you look them in the eye or do you turn away quickly? You may not even realize you are doing this. The message you are sending is a lack of confidence.

When our belief system and thought patterns are not serving us in a favorable way, we must know that they can be changed. However, these habits have been instilled in us since childhood and don't easily go away. It takes time to create new habits and ways of thinking. Working with a coach over a period of time can shift the patterns and change the way you see yourself. Your confidence will increase and lead to more successful business deals.

One of the best books I recommend you read on this subject is "*Nice Girl's Don't Get The Corner Office: 101 Unconscious Mistakes Women Make That Sabotage Their Careers*" by Louis P. Frankel. PhD. It is one of the books we review in the Infinity Coaching Inner Circle to strengthen our leadership skill sets.

Going it alone. There will be people who do not support you on your entrepreneurial path. Some of these people may even be those that are close to you. A close friend, family member or even an entrepreneur you may have known for some time. My father did not support me.

My father didn't want me to start a business. I remember him telling me, I was doing this for some type of fame. He wanted me to take the safe route and get a government job or work with a contractor after I retired. I actually turned down two positions with very nice salaries. I may not have known much about starting a business but I knew what I didn't want, and that was half the battle won.

During the start-up years when my business was not earning much income, I had a few friends say to walk away. One even said I don't think this is what God has in store for you. Ouch! I didn't have the support of my family or a few of my close friends. It didn't mean they didn't care. They just did not share my dream and vision. I ended up taking a few bumpy roads before I found my tribe that would lead me to my path of success. A coach can provide that sounding board you need. A coach will be the nonjudgmental, motivating voice that can help you face your challenges and fears. They will assist you with moving out of your comfort zone and break through whatever is holding you back.

Not letting go and delegating. You are used to going it alone, having to get it all done, and you carry this belief into your business. A strong, effective leader knows how to delegate effectively. You are going to find, if you haven't already, there are things you are stronger at and things you are weaker at. Let go of the things that you are weak at, and let someone else take on those responsibilities.

For many, it's hard to let go and they often view a project as their baby – no one will do it as good as they will. This can be exhausting! Not letting go can impede productivity, as you spend way too much time on the minor details, worrying about every little detail. Often these tasks can easily be handled by someone else. The stress of holding on tightly to a task can eventually lead to health issues such as heart disease.

Many people hate to admit there are some things they just don't do as well. Working with a coach can help you face yourself and identify your strengths and weaknesses. You can identify which tasks you can delegate and develop an effective strategy for doing so. Your time will be free to focus on the business aspects you enjoy doing leading to increased productivity and revenue. An added bonus, you stay out of the hospital.

Not saying No. "No" is one of the most powerful words in the English language, actually in any language for that matter. As powerful as the word is, we, especially as women, don't say it enough. So much so we will let our businesses suffer while we attend to the needs, dreams, and desires of everyone around us. If we say "yes" to ourselves and/or our business, we tend to feel we are just being selfish. This is what we have been taught to believe.

In order for your business to survive, you are going to have to learn to say "no." You will have to learn how to set boundaries and run your business like a business. This may mean setting working hours so your friends and families learn to respect that just like they have their careers, this is the time when you are conducting business.

Take a look at your day and see how you are spending your time. Are you doing things that are not in alignment with your business goals? What are you saying "yes" to when you don't mean it? You may find you are doing things not because you want to, but because you feel obligated to.

Working with a coach, you can clearly identify your priorities and create daily action steps. I had the habit of saying yes to everyone's project but my own. When I started listing my priorities and holding myself accountable each week, I saw significant growth in my business. I now teach this strategy to clients I work with.

Get Support. I could have easily put all of this under the section Going It Alone, but I wanted to put extra emphasis on the need for support. I mentioned earlier that many women do not know much about coaching. Many women who transition from the workforce to entrepreneurship also have never had a mentor in the workplace, let alone as a business owner. In male-dominated industries, men often feel uncomfortable or don't know how to mentor women. When you are sharing some of the things you are experiencing, they just don't get it.

Now don't take this the wrong way. I am not saying men cannot mentor or coach women. Nor am I saying you should not have a male mentor or coach. You have met a few excellent, highly recommended males coaches in this book. This is just the reality of many women's collective experience.

Many women have never experienced what it is like

receiving support for their career. These feelings carry over into the business you are starting and you adopt an "I have to do it all" mentality. As a business owner, you wear many hats. One day, just write it all down. Write down all the things you do on a given day. Don't just write down the professional stuff, write down all the personal stuff too. Write down everything. Then ask yourself, and be honest, how long can you keep going at that pace?

Women struggle with asking for help. They are used to being the one providing the help and resources for others. It's almost a Superwoman syndrome that we can and have to be everything to everybody. Even in our darkest hours, we don't ask for help. To succeed in business, you will have to learn to let go of this way of thinking. A coach can help you develop a plan so you can delegate, be organized and know when to ask for help. If you are not comfortable asking for help, your coach will work with you so you will become comfortable. Doing so will reduce stress and lead to greater productivity.

I am of the belief that every entrepreneur should have a coach appropriate for the level they are at in their business. Why? Because coaching works! There is a lot of free stuff out there you can download from the Internet and there are tons of online courses you can buy. Trust me, I have bought my share of them.

Can you learn from these programs? Yes, you can. But I wasted a lot of time and money not knowing what I really needed. I got sucked into the world of quick results - if you do it just like me for a small, sometimes large investment, you too can have the same results. Have you seen those ads? Had I been working with a coach, I could have saved a lot of money. Now I work with my coaching clients to help them from making some of the same mistakes I made.

Finding a coach that fits your needs can be challenging. If a coach tells you, "I can work with everybody", I would be a bit sceptical. The client-coaching relationship is just that, a relationship. If you look at in terms of dating, you don't want to date everyone you meet do you? So how do you know what's right for you? Keep these suggestions in mind when looking for YOUR coach.

Have a complimentary session first. You should always meet with a potential coach before investing. You want to understand their approach to coaching. This may not apply to an online course you are purchasing unless the course is a significant investment. Most coaches will offer a complimentary session. If they don't, ask for one.

Use this initial time to assess and see if you are compatible; is this someone you feel comfortable working with? Are they making promises that seem too good to be true? If they are, beware. No coach should guarantee anything or make promises that are unrealistic.

Clarify what you will receive during the coaching process. How often will you meet? How long will the sessions be? Do you need a coach who works weekends or evenings; not all coaches do. What is the cost of the sessions?

When it comes to cost, you may have heard the expression, what you pay for is what you get. Some people are of the belief that if you pay more for coaching, you will get the best top-quality coaching experience. This is not always the case. I know several entrepreneurs who paid exorbitant, ridiculous amounts of money for coaching and a year later, their business had not grown. They were not even in revenue. Do your research about the coach and look at similar programs to compare cost. I encourage all of my clients, before they hire me, to do their homework. This way they know they are getting valuable, high-quality coaching.

Just like Me. Some people are of the perspective their coach needs to be just like them. They need to have the same background, work experience and come from the same part of the world. It is okay if you have a few commonalities, but if you are too similar, you can run into roadblocks with your coaching. The coach may have the same bias and filters you have. They will agree and sympathize far too much. Instead of moving forward, you can remain stuck. Or you may end up in an even deeper situation than before.

In order for the coaching process to be effective, the coach does not have to be like you. Having a different life experience enables them to serve you better. They will be able to see things from a different perspective, allowing you to see past the filters and biases you have.

Establish Trust. Trust is integral to the coaching relationship. You need to feel comfortable with your coach. When I first started my coaching business, I spent time in a group coaching program to see what it was like. During the initial call, the coach leading the program provided additional information and I was very excited to join the group.

A few months into the program, the material that was being presented was not what was discussed with me. What was being presented went against a core belief of mine. I was able to speak with her and explain my concerns. She wanted me to try something first before she considered allowing me to leave the group, which I agreed to do. What she asked me to do ended up being very similar to the other experience, further violating the trust.

Even with this second incident, she was not going to approve me leaving the group. This meant I would continue to be charged the monthly fee for the next nine months. I asked how could she, as the coach, have this attitude when she violated my trust a second time after trying to resolve the situation. After consulting with colleagues and some reflection, she agreed to cancel the membership. She understood she had violated the trust we had established and agreed it was the best solution.

I share this story with you not to say "Wow, look what this

coach did!" but for you to truly understand the importance of trust in the coaching relationship. How would I feel comfortable getting on the group calls? How would I be able to trust my coach? If at any time, you feel as if a coach you are working with is not upholding the agreement you have made, you must speak up. I know women who did not. They ended up not participating, continuing to pay for a program with someone who had violated their trust. There was no gain for them. No personal or professional growth. You do not have to do this. If it is not working out, speak with the coach and end the coaching relationship.

As a coach, I put a clause in my coaching agreements, stating the client is to let me know if I am not meeting expectations. If I am not, we can discuss how we change things or I can refer them to someone else. I have never had a client who needed to do this, but for me, it is important to honor and protect the rights of all my clients. Trust and confidentiality are two things I value highly in the client-coach relationship. So should any coach you choose to work with.

Group vs 1:1 Coaching. Many coaches offer only one-on-one coaching, group coaching, or both. One-on-one coaching can be a bit more expensive so you have to decide what is best for your learning style. For me, when I was focused on a particular goal, one-on-one worked better. I have clients who will only work with me one-on-one. The advantage is the individual, structured attention and focus. You work closely with your coach to achieve your goals and create a strategy.

With group coaching, you are able to meet and connect with individuals with goals that are very similar to yours. These groups are typically referred to as an Inner Circle or Mastermind group. You learn from each other, sharing stories and experiences that can also stir your creativity. The discussions are facilitated and often open with the coach sharing a lesson on a particular subject. I have seen many businesses and lives changed using this method. I facilitate the Infinity Coaching Inner Circle, an elite career and leadership community. It is an exclusive group which provides you access to expert teaching, coaching and mentoring. You can find out more about the program at www.infinitycoaching.net/innercircle.

Take time to see what program fits your needs. You may find you prefer a combination of one-on-one and group coaching. Do your due diligence first and ask the right questions to know what is best for you.

I want to share with you something that happened to me and why paying attention to these strategies is so important. As an entrepreneur, I believe it is important to have a presence on social media. As a Social Media Career Strategist, I even assist my clients with getting started on key platforms. While working with one of my coaches, I learned he did not support using social media to grow your business. He accepted the fact I did, or at least that was what I was initially led to believe.

Over time he became very verbal of his dislike for it and criticized me very harshly for doing so. I would feel awful after some of the coaching sessions. Not from growing personally or professionally but from the constant criticism from my coach. Criticism because of something he did not believe in. He did not respect my desire to try something I believed would truly help my business grow. The criticism grew into other areas as well. Needless to say, we ended the coaching relationship early.

When I look back on this experience, I learned I could have asked better questions. I could have done the appropriate research before agreeing to hire him. But, I did not let it deter me from moving forward and finding another coach. I was able to identify what type of coaching I needed, started asking the right questions before I hired someone and that made all the difference for my business. I found a coach who helped me raise the game in my business. She and I are still friends today. Oh, and on a separate note, from my presence on social media, I have received opportunities for joint ventures, interviews and job offers. Glad I didn't listen to him!

In this book, you have been introduced to some amazing coaches. All offer unique skills sets and different approaches to coaching. Don't be overwhelmed by the contents. You don't have to dash through and accomplish everything you have read or will read immediately. The common thread we all want you to understand, is the need for entrepreneurs to have a coach, especially when starting their business. It is even more important for women to recognize the value of coaching and how it can play an integral, important role in growing your business.

Have you heard the saying, "Behind every good man, is a good woman"? I like to say, "Behind every good woman is a Sisterhood". The world of entrepreneurship can be a lonely, overwhelming and stressful place. Building any business takes hard work. It takes time and patience. Surround yourself with sisters who are entrepreneurs and coaches who are there to support you along this marvellous journey. The reward is truly worth it.

If you would like to learn more about the services and programs I offer or if I can be of any assistance to you during your journey, please reach out to me at cowens@infinitycoaching. It is truly a gift to serve my clients, helping them take their dreams and ideas and turn them into reality. *Here's to your success!*

About the Author

Carolyn R. Owens is a retired United States Navy Commander, Amazon #1 Best Selling Author and President and Founder of Infinity Coaching, Inc. A leading authority on leadership and professional development, Carolyn uses principles derived from the world's most respected military training programs to educate and train top leaders and business owners across the globe. She works with her clients to awaken their self-awareness so they can achieve greater communication, interaction and engagement with their customers, clients and teams as well as in their personal relationships.

During her military career, she served as the Director of Human Capital Management for an organization of over 4,800 civilian, military and contract personnel. Her favorite assignment was when she served as a Professor in the Department of Command Leadership and Management at the United States Army War College. Upon retiring from the military, she decided to turn the part she loved most into a second career and Infinity Coaching, Inc. was born.

Carolyn served as the President of the Maryland Career Development Association and is the host of the podcast, "Let's Coach". She has been featured in Money Magazine, Fox News Magazine, Huffington Post, YourTango, Legacy in the Making Magazine, and many other publications. She serves as a guest speaker for conferences and seminars, which has included the American Psychological Association (APA) Career Fair and the Maryland Counseling Association Conference. She is a frequent guest expert on local and national radio shows.

Having served in key leadership positions and as a successful business owner, Carolyn knows quite well some of the challenges one faces when pursuing the career and life of their dreams. The company she founded, Infinity Coaching, Inc., provides career, executive and leadership coaching that moves individuals forward, allowing them to take COMMAND of their lives.

To raise your awareness about your leadership skills visit http://leadershipmasteryassessment.com/ for a free assessment. You will quickly discover areas you are performing well in as well as areas that may need additional attention. This will enable you to clearly define your goals and achieve a life you truly desire. It's all about having success on YOUR own terms!

Carolyn R Owens, ACC, CPC, SPHR
Certified Career Strategist, Leadership and Life Coach
www.infinitycoaching.net
cowens@infinitycoaching.net

Connect with Carolyn on social media:
Twitter: www.twitter.com/CarolROwens
LinkedIn: www.linkedin.com/in/cowensinfinitycoaching
Facebook: www.facebook.com/infinitycoaching.co
Instagram: www.instagram.com/carolynrowens

Hope, Possibilities, and Empowerment
By Deborah Jane Wells

I'm sometimes asked if, as a life coach and female entrepreneur, I coach business situations. Yes, I coach everything, because life includes everything. I hold multiple professional coaching certifications, including board certification. I'm also retired from a thirty-year consulting career specializing in human resources and organization transformation, including serving as a senior partner in four of the world's largest and most prestigious global professional services firms. By virtue of my experience and expertise, I am well qualified to coach entrepreneurs, executives and professionals at all levels concerning a multitude of business situations.

Going beyond qualifications, the real answer is that life is just life. Despite our best efforts to separate our work and personal lives, those boundaries prove artificial, superficial, and highly permeable. Whether a client comes to me wanting help with a work situation or a personal relationship, inevitably, the lines blur. Wherever you go, there you are. How you do anything is how you do everything.

When we choose fear as our fuel, any of us—individuals and organizations alike—can become stuck in the "hamster wheel" approach to life. Trapped by the mistaken belief that busyness is the same as purpose, we can't stand the way we're living but feel powerless to change.

As we work together, my clients discover what I discovered: when you fall in love with yourself, everything else falls into place, personally and professionally. Choosing love as your core energy automatically enhances every aspect of your life: your perceptions, opportunities, relationships, and priorities. You get unstuck, reclaim your personal power, and recapture your zest for living, moving yourself forward into a life you love. When love transforms your relationship with yourself, it transforms your personal life, your work, and the world.

It all starts with embracing the amazing and liberating possibility that the love of your life just might be YOU. Many people tell me it feels selfish to think in those terms. That we are supposed to love and care for "our neighbor." I remind them we are also supposed to "love our neighbor as ourselves." Many of us would end up in court or prison if we treated our neighbors the way we treat ourselves.

When we spend our lives not taking care of ourselves, eventually we are no good to ourselves or anyone else. We cannot share anything of lasting value with others by giving from an empty well. When we learn to treat ourselves with love, respect, curiosity, compassion, and gratitude in each and every moment, then, and only then, will we find ourselves able to be of genuine service to others.

The lessons that follow explore some of the shared challenges that female entrepreneurs encounter and the mindset and behavioral shifts that help them, not just survive, but thrive!

The Lesson of Core Strength

According to fitness experts, many people are not familiar with the term "core strength training" or they think it refers only to six-pack abs. Sports Fitness Advisor's description is much broader:

> Core strength training may be a relatively new, buzz term in the fitness industry but coaches and athletes have understood its value for many years. The core region consists of far more than just the abdominal muscles. In fact core strength training aims to target all the muscle groups that stabilize the spine and pelvis. It's these muscle groups that are critical for the transfer of energy from large to small body parts during many sporting activities (2013).

My client Lori could easily be a poster child for core training. She works out at the gym regularly, not to mention completing sixty-mile bike rides on the weekends and a run along the water several times a week. Even so, in Lori's book, real core strength training takes more than cardio, abs, and back work. In her words, "The real core is even further in."

While many might be envious of Lori's healthy weight and physical fitness, she's a perfect example that being lean and fit is not a guarantee for feeling fulfilled and whole.

If you encountered Lori in person, you would see a smart, successful, attractive woman who appears to have it all together. You might even feel a twinge of resentment that she makes it look so easy, but her genuine thoughtfulness, authenticity, and gentle heart are irresistible. Those who know her well marvel that she retains that authentic kindness in the face of the challenges she has experienced over the years.

At one point, Lori was on the verge of bankruptcy, having gone from an extraordinary net worth to serious trouble. It certainly wasn't from excessive spending or waste. Lori was always a saver and independently built her net worth through hard work and successful investments. Prior to the US economic meltdown, her years of careful saving and frugal living were paying off. Then, overnight, the real estate crisis transformed many of her investments from assets to liabilities.

During that difficult time, a man who had been her friend for ten years became more, and they moved in together. It's amazing what you discover when you live with someone. Over time, it became obvious to her that even a long-term friendship did not necessarily segue into a healthy intimate relationship. Even so, she didn't give up easily. Her nature is to assess any problem and try to fix it, even if the problem lies well outside her control.

The one-two punch of devastating financial results and a deeply disappointing relationship took a toll on core strengths that had long enabled Lori to quickly solve problems and put things right. The most devastating casualty was a loss of trust in herself. That distrust began spreading like a virus until she was questioning not just her financial and relationship judgment but nearly every decision she faced.

Eventually, the level of her personal discomfort told her things had to change. But she couldn't seem to find her way back to trusting herself and knowing she was "enough." At the recommendation of a friend, Lori visited my website and read the success stories of others who had worked with me.

"I finally recognized that I needed a 'tune-up,'" Lori said. "I had paid attention to personal growth for many years, immersing myself in the work of Dr. Wayne W. Dyer, Deepak Chopra, and others. Nonetheless, somehow I had somehow gotten off track.

"My first conversation with Deborah 'sold me.' Step-by-step, our work together provided me with much-needed course corrections to deal with the distrust and discomfort I was feeling. I learned that recognizing those feelings and dealing with them was an important first step toward the changes I desired. Carving the time for coaching out of my endless to-do list was an important commitment to and investment in my relationship with myself."

Somewhere along the way, Lori stopped trusting herself and started measuring herself by other people's opinions and standards. We talked at length about the five agreements of spiritual teacher and author don Miguel Ruiz based on ancient Toltec wisdom. In his book *The Fifth Agreement* (2010), he suggests using doubt as a tool to discern the truth. He wisely counsels never to treat what is true for someone else as your personal truth; instead, listen with respect, curiosity, and discernment. There is no need to be afraid of listening to others, since you always have the ability to apply your own discernment and determine if what you hear resonates with *your* truth. Connecting deeply with others allows for the possibility that they will awaken within you a *personal truth* that lies sleeping.

Suddenly the fact that Lori had doubts about herself was not necessarily a problem but a gift. Lori found the strength to terminate the relationship that was sapping her energy and eroding her confidence. She took thoughtful, careful, gentle steps that led to a compassionate and clean break. Her relief at "getting herself back" was powerful and palpable.

"Deborah is a night light. She shines light on the dark places. She walks with you, she holds your hand, but she won't, she can't, do the work for you. If you have the courage and commitment to get up and walk—to do the hard work of changing—your journey will be incredibly rewarding. Deborah will help you strengthen your 'core' quicker than any ab exercise out there.

"The most important change I've made is turning my focus inward for answers and strength. I needed to be reminded not to look to others to convince me of my own value."

When Lori said "the real core is even further in," she was referring to the fact that long before a "strong core" described physical fitness, the term was used to describe a different kind of strength. The strength it takes to trust yourself, to find wisdom within, and to live by the light of your own truth.

As Lori continues to live her truth, her self-confidence, self-esteem, and finances continue to improve. She is making clear choices about everything from her career to a long-troubled relationship with her parents. She has begun fostering a guide dog for a local charity—a long-buried desire that has the potential to bring self-fulfillment, laughter, and energy into her life. Until she honored and made room for it, that dream had remained a quiet wish that sat in her heart, waiting for its time to come.

Core Concepts
In "The Lesson of Core Strength," Lori discovered:
- When we don't remain mindful, setbacks and disappointments can cause us to lose faith in our own intuition and reasoning and think that others know better than we do how we should live our lives.
- Never automatically treat what is true for someone else as your personal truth; instead, listen to others with respect, curiosity, and discernment.

- There is no need to be afraid of listening to others, since you always have the ability to apply your own discernment and determine if what you hear resonates with your truth.
- Connecting deeply with others allows for the possibility that they will awaken within you a personal truth that lies sleeping.

Reflection
- What do you think about the possibility that, when things don't turn out as you'd planned, giving up on yourself and playing it small is not the optimal response?
- What feelings arise when you consider listening to others during times of disappointment and frustration and then going within to connect deeply with your personal truth?

Opportunities
- Where specifically is a pattern of not trusting your own deepest wisdom keeping you trapped in a cycle of self-doubt and misery?
- If you were able to love yourself unconditionally and respect that you are always doing the best you can with the love and light you have at the time, how might you rebuild your confidence and find the courage to begin anew?

The Lesson of Behave As If
The behave-as-if principle says that one potential way to create the new behaviors, environments, relationships, and feelings we want is to *behave as if* they were already present.

This approach goes much deeper than the popular "fake it till you make it" idea. If you give serious thought to how you would like your life to feel, a key component in making it a reality might be a specific set of characteristics and behaviors you would need to exhibit to make it happen. You might even find that those characteristics already exist as a cultural role model.

If, as Willie Nelson sings in his 1980 hit, your "heroes have always been cowboys" and you were trying to shape yourself into that ideal image, there are some things you might emulate and others you might avoid. For example, you might attend the rodeo, take horseback riding lessons, and wear flannel shirts, jeans, and boots. On the other hand, you probably wouldn't wear pink, eat tofu, or read *Oprah Magazine*.

Your cowboy role model would become a lens through which your choices would become obvious and well within your control. You could begin modifying your "packaging," skills, and actions to behave your way closer to how you'd like to feel and show up in life. As your external attributes begin to align with your ideal image, those initial successes would reinforce your belief that you *can* succeed, providing just the positive energy boost you may need to make it the rest of the way to achieving your ultimate goal.

My client Betty worked with me on using the behave-as-if principle to help her transform some of her self-sabotaging thought and behavior patterns. If you were to meet Betty, it would never occur to you that she was a person with confidence problems. She greets the world with a cheerful smile and the appearance of a solid professional, sure of her ability and her unique skill set.

The reality, however, is that she has a vision of how she'd like to show up in her life and she thus far feels that she hasn't been able to fit herself inside that particular skin.

When she considers why that is, Betty comes back to an idea that is all too common: she does a great job of taking care of, honoring, and watching over the other people in her life, but she herself falls far down on her priority list. In fact, if *she* wanted to be a cowboy, she probably wouldn't even make time to buy herself a pair of jeans. Meanwhile, she would make sure her children and clients had everything they needed to grow into their best selves.

Like so many of us, the great irony was that Betty didn't need an external role model after which to pattern her transition to her ideal image. The behaviors Betty desired were already well within her core strengths. It just wasn't occurring to her to apply them to meeting her own needs. In the words of Malcolm S. Forbes, "Too many people overvalue what they are not and undervalue what they are."

Using the behave-as-if principle can be a great way to get a new habit going and convince ourselves we have what it takes to go the distance. One of the ways she follows through on meeting the needs of her family and clients is to post reminder notes in places she can't miss. As a result of our work together, she has started posting notes all over her house reminding herself to notice and commit to meeting her needs and desires as well.

The benefits of learning to love herself have turned Betty into a strong advocate for this complex and rewarding work. "As a result of what I've learned in coaching with Deborah, I've engaged a colleague to serve as an 'accountability partner,'" she said. "I wanted a peer whose work is totally different from mine and who, like me, is willing to be held accountable and meet commitments not only to our clients and our families but to ourselves.

"Recently I started a newsletter for my clients. In the second issue, I talked about the importance of taking care of ourselves as well as we take care of everyone else in our lives. I shared my personal story with my clients, including the powerful return on investment I have received from investing my time, effort, and resources in working with a life coach. I know many of my clients will resonate with my story. My willingness to share it in an authentic way will likely open the door to even more powerful conversations between us."

As Elisabeth Kübler-Ross put it, "People are like stained-glass windows. They sparkle and shine when the sun is out, but when the darkness sets in their true beauty is revealed only if there is light from within."

A powerful way to turn on the light of love within you and keep it burning brightly is to ask yourself many times each day, "If I were my own beloved child or valued client, how would I take care of *me* right now?"

Core Concepts
In "The Lesson of Behave As If," Betty discovered:
- In "The Lesson of Behave As If," Betty discovered:
- When we spend our lives not taking care of ourselves, eventually we are no good to ourselves or anyone else.
- We cannot share anything of lasting value with others by giving from an empty well.
- Using the behave-as-if principle can be a great way to get a new habit going and convince ourselves we have what it takes to go the distance.
- When we learn to treat ourselves with love in every moment, then—and only then—will we find ourselves able to be of genuine service to others.
- A powerful way to turn on the light of love within you and keep it burning brightly is to ask yourself many times each day, "If I were my own beloved child or valued client, how would I take care of me right now?"

Reflection
- What do you think about the possibility that taking care of yourself is the least selfish thing you can do?
- What feelings arise when you consider demonstrating unconditional love, respect, and compassion for yourself in each moment and making self-care a priority?

Opportunities
- Where specifically is a pattern of ignoring self-care keeping you stuck in a way of living that is burning you out?
- If you really began recognizing, respecting, and valuing your health and welfare—physically, mentally, emotionally, and spiritually—what first step might you take toward better investing in your highest good by treating yourself like your own beloved child?

The Lesson of Connection
Imagine for a moment that you are a satellite. In the silence and the darkness of space, you regularly receive and transmit information to Earth. The communication works smoothly most of the time, and

even if your signal is sometimes disrupted temporarily, the disruption rarely lasts very long.

You go on your way, secure in your orbit and in who and what you are. Until something happens to disrupt your orbit or positioning significantly. In space, it could be a blast of excess energy from the sun.

For a satellite that is turned away from its source, there is no option except to begin transmitting "Lost Earth" repeatedly, with no assurance the signal will ever be heard.

Those melancholy words, "Lost Earth," reflect disconnection from the only Source the satellite "knows."

Unlike a satellite, when something disrupts our "orbit" and connections to our Source, we might not even recognize that we are no longer communicating with our authentic self. In life, it could be a serious illness, a job loss, or just too many little challenges at one time. Unlike the satellite, our "programming" may keep us from crying out for help.

Over time, if the connection between how we show up in the world and who we are at our core becomes weaker and weaker, our personal orbit becomes askew, and only a significant repositioning can put us back in touch and back on track. Meanwhile — during the time of that disconnection — the darkness and the silence within can become as profound as the vast darkness and silence of outer space.

By now, you may be wondering what all this has to do with life coaching. When I met my client Cecilia, an expert in satellite technology, she described herself as having "Lost Earth." She realized that over a period of years she had faced away, or disconnected, from her authentic self. With her wry sense of humor, she wondered if anyone would notice or try to assist her if she walked around saying, "Lost Earth."

What does it look like when we disconnect from our essential, authentic selves? To an outside observer, it might look like life on a hamster wheel—busy, busy, busy. No longer spending time doing things we used to love, like music, art, or outdoor activities.

Those pastimes or passions slip away, quietly, slowly. We are stuck out there in the darkness and the silence. The external self has turned away and cannot see or "receive" from the authentic self any longer.

Cecilia didn't disconnect from her true self because of solar flares or solar wind. Instead, she disconnected for the same reasons many of us do: physical, mental, emotional, and spiritual burnout.

This kind of disconnection rarely happens overnight. It is more likely to creep up on us over time as life becomes increasingly complex. It might start with putting a spouse through law school and then dealing with marital problems, a divorce, a complex demanding job, and constant business travel. All of this continues until there is so little left of the authentic self and its many strengths that the next thing that comes along is just one thing too many. Staying connected to your authentic self is not just a nice thing to do. It is essential.

In Cecilia's case, the one thing too many was becoming responsible for a father with multiple illnesses, including one that was slowly robbing him of his vision. As his health continued to decline, her responsibilities continued to escalate with exhausting complexity. Move him into assisted living. Deal with the realtors. Arrange for the sale of his house. Make sure his taxes were paid. Meet with his doctors. Make critical health care decisions.

At some point she made a conscious decision that she "didn't have time" for anything but work and her father. She consciously placed the things that brought her joy and were at the heart of her truest self on a back burner. She was just too busy to take care of herself too.

But even after her father died, nothing changed. She found herself still too busy, even though her responsibilities on his behalf had diminished to serving as executor of his estate. She was out of the real estate business and the health care business but was immersed instead in the business of wrapping up someone else's life.

By this time, she knew she needed help. She had worked with an iPEC life coach once before and knew that help was out there somewhere. One day she started actively looking. Her "Lost Earth" signal was going to be transmitted at last. In Cecilia's words, "I didn't want to talk about my feelings; I wanted to know what I could do to change my life." Having experienced an iPEC coach in the past, she started by researching coaches on iPEC's website. As it happened, I was their featured coach that day.

We connected through my life coaching website and set up a sixty-minute complimentary session. Our conversation revealed that we had more in common than living in Colorado. Many of the aspects of Cecilia's authentic self that had been left by the wayside were alive and well in me. A love of music, creative endeavors, and helping others provided a strong basis for connection between us. In the years leading up to my own burnout, I too had left them by the side of the road, too busy with work and taking care of everyone else to realize the long-term damage that would result.

"Deborah's ability to get to the core of an issue just takes my breath away. Her insight distills things down to the simple truth—a truth clear enough for you to work with and through. She provides tools to help me navigate and re-connect with my authentic self. Don't be surprised if you start by focusing in one area of your life, only to make deeper, more profound discoveries and changes in other aspects of your life as well."

As we worked together, Cecilia began to rebuild her own internal connections. Little by little, her "lost" self re-emerged. At her optometrist's office, she "happened" to notice the collection of ukuleles and asked about buying one and learning to play it.

"Life coaching gave me tools to help me navigate my life. When you have 'Lost Earth' and lost your way, what you need most is a new way to navigate." Once she got started, Cecilia learned to set her intention and tap into more and more of her authentic self. Beyond the rediscovery of her joy in music and quilting, she began looking seriously at what she'd like to do when she retires. How could she prepare? What might she bring to the next chapter of her life in light of all she had learned?

Today she has a business model and website that will help her assist other women in using creativity to deal with some of the challenges she has faced. She is fully engaged with a new vision of her future and has new tools to help her should she ever find that she has once again, even momentarily, "Lost Earth."

Core Concepts
In "The Lesson of Connection," Cecilia discovered:
- When something disrupts our "orbit" and connections to our Source, we might not even recognize that we are no longer communicating with our authentic self.
- Often, when we become obsessed with working and taking care of everyone else, we fail to realize the long-term damage that will result to our health and zest for living.
- This kind of disconnection rarely happens overnight. It is more likely to creep up on us over time as life becomes increasingly complex.
- When you have lost your way, what you need most is a new way to navigate.
- Staying connected to your authentic self through rest, reflection and play is not just a nice thing to do. It's essential.

Reflection
- What do you think about the likelihood that burnout will occur whenever we choose to live the hamster wheel life with no commitment to our own health and welfare?
- What feelings arise when you consider investing more of your energy in nurturing, encouraging, and delighting yourself in healthy ways rather than working constantly and only taking care of others?

Opportunities
- Where specifically might a habit of overworking and overcommitting be contributing to a pattern of burning

yourself out physically, mentally, emotionally, and spiritually?

- How specifically might you begin infusing your life with more creativity and fun? How might doing so bring you renewed energy, joy, and fulfillment?

Conclusion and Commitment

It is interesting that those who learn to fall in love with themselves are actually less likely to behave selfishly. Their joy and peace are contagious. They show up in their families, workplaces, and friendships with a spring in their step and a zest for living that carries them, and those around them, forward in new and exciting directions.

Bottom line? It's not just okay to fall in love with yourself. It's essential.

When you fall in love with yourself, everything else finally falls into place. This transformation arises from a fundamental shift in your head and heart. Once love transforms your relationship with yourself, it can't help but transform your personal life and work in ways that will exhilarate you. Your more constructive personal energy will automatically transform every being and situation you encounter. You will, by your very presence, quite literally, transform the world.

What small step will you take to begin moving forward into a life you love? And who might you engage to provide moral support and hold you accountable? You've got nothing to lose, except the limits fear, stress, and pain have been placing on your life. Time to get off that hamster wheel and step into your greatness.

About the Author

As a board-certified coach, author, and Reiki master teacher, Deborah Jane Wells shares hope, possibilities, and empowerment with the world. What's love got to do with minimizing stress and getting unstuck? Everything! Her book, *Choose Your Energy: Change Your Life!* (Hay House/Balboa Press 2013) shares her story and the stories of 10 of her clients along with her signature Discovery Framework.

During her 30 years as an organization transformation consultant, Deborah served as a senior partner in four of the world's largest, most prestigious global professional services firms. In 2005, she took a five-year sabbatical to find healing and peace because non-stop work had taken its toll. Her recovery from burnout, including a sustained 80-pound weight loss and freedom from 10 years of debilitating depression, led to finding her purpose sharing hope, possibilities, and empowerment with the world.

Through healing and self-exploration, Deborah discovered that loving yourself unconditionally is the key to transforming your personal life, your work, and the world. With attention and intention, she learned to live in alignment with love through a wealth of energy-shifting tools and techniques that help her reduce stress, anxiety, and overwhelm by releasing limiting beliefs, emotions, and habits.

Deborah's books, blog, radio show, and signature coaching programs help individuals and organizations harness the transformative energy of love to turn unexplored possibilities into fulfilling realities and step into their greatness. To learn more about her work in the world, visit http://djwlifecoach.com.

For fun, Deborah loves singing, reading, sewing, knitting, golfing, and movies. She lives in Williamsburg, Virginia with her husband, Wilson, and the coaching cats who manage her life—SiddhaLee and Maisy Jane.

The International Association of Professional Life Coaches® (IAPLC)

Visibility ~ Credibility ~ Connection

The IAPLC is an organization for life coaches to list their services and for others to find a life coach. Members must meet certain criteria to be listed. As an international professional association dedicated exclusively to the life coaching industry it has membership standards based on training, coaching experience and client references.

To find a life coach: Our user-friendly online directory has listings of life coaches in over 15 different categories. Anyone seeking a life coach will find all the information they need to aid them in selecting a coach.

The directory can be found at www.iaplifecoaches.org/life-coach-directory

To download our "Find a Coach Guide" go to: www.iaplifecoaches.org/find-a-coach/

To become a member: The association combines a premier user-friendly international online directory with group business-building activities for its members so they can grow their coaching businesses and get more clients.

To become a member, visit: www.iaplifecoaches.org

Made in the USA
Middletown, DE
28 December 2017